BASIC BIBL [P9-COO-698]

PHILIPPIANS

JOY
IN THE
LORD

DAVID C. COOK PUBLISHING CO.
ELGIN, IL 60120

This Basic Bible Series study was developed through the combined efforts and resources of a number of David C. Cook's dedicated lesson writers. It was compiled and edited by Roger Searle, designed by Melanie Lawson and Dawn Lauck, with cover art by Richard Sparks.
—Gary Wilde, Series Editor

Philippians: Joy in the Lord

© 1986 David C. Cook Publishing Co., 850 North Grove Ave., Elgin, IL 60120. Printed in U.S.A.

Scripture quotations, unless otherwise noted, are taken from the Holy Bible: New International Version, © 1973, 1978, 1984 by the International Bible Society, used by permission of Zondervan Bible Publishers.

ISBN: 0-89191-482-X
Library of Congress Catalog Number: 86-70883

Philippians 1:25

For your progress and joy in the faith.

Contents

1

Introducing the Book of Philippians

Truth to Apply: The awesome power of God is at work in me as I submit to the Spirit's leading.

Key Verse: The whole family was filled with joy, because they had come to believe in God (Acts 16:34b).

Three major miracles prepared the way for the founding of the Philippian church: the Macedonian vision, the healing of the demon-possessed girl, and the miracle in the Philippian jail. Each one was God's intervening in a person's life. With this evidence of God's working, the church remained faithful to the Gospel, and in partnership with Paul. In what ways have you experienced the "miraculous" in your own life?

The Town of Philippi

Paul had already made a church-planting trip, starting churches in Antioch of Pisidia, Iconium, Lystra, and other places. His second journey started out as simply a return visit to some of the churches to encourage them and see how they were doing. At this time Paul and Barnabas had their "falling out" (Acts 15:36), so Paul and Silas (along with Timothy and possibly Luke) set out to visit the churches.

The group found themselves in Troas, unsure of God's will for their journey's direction. Twice doors had been closed while they were trying to spread the Gospel (east to Asia and North to Bithynia).

Finally, the doorway to Macedonia opened through Paul's vision of a man from Macedonia saying, "Come over to Macedonia and help us." This vivid example of God's leading drew a quick response. They set out "at once" (Acts 16:10).

Paul and his group crossed the Aegean Sea to Neapolis, a seaport of Philippi. Named for the father of Alexander the Great (Philip), Philippi was founded in the fourth century B.C. as a gold and silver mining center. Located on the great Egnatian Road where the Balkan mountains form a pass, the city was a strategic outpost.

A Roman colony, Philippi had organized itself as a miniature Rome, complete with Roman citizens who wore Roman clothes, copied Roman society, and followed Roman law. It enjoyed the benefits of peace, stable government, active trade, and good transportation. Paul was taking Christ's Gospel into the most important and strategic city in the area!

New Beginning

Paul's first European convert was Lydia, a businesswoman from Thyatira. Lydia made her living selling valuable purple cloth colored with dye obtained from shellfish.

Significantly, Paul found her worshiping in a Jewish prayer meeting. Evidently a convert to Judaism, Lydia was a serious, devout woman worshiping God the best way she knew how. When she heard the Gospel message,

Lydia and her entire household were baptized by Paul. After opening her heart to Christ, Lydia opened her home to Paul and his group. Her house became a haven to the evangelists in a hostile city, and became a meeting place for the first Philippian believers.

The Jailer and the Jailed (Acts 16)

When Paul healed a demon-possessed woman her employers became angry. They had Paul and Silas beaten and thrown into prison. With hands and feet in stocks, backs bleeding, the two missionaries were truly suffering for Christ's sake.

In the midst of an ugly Philippian jail, these two ministers of the Gospel were able to pray and praise God. Their singing was heard throughout the jail. The other prisoners were a captive audience to the testimony of God's sustaining grace. Cursesthey could understand—but whoever heard of bleeding prisoners sounding so happy?

When God's earthquake loosened the stocks and prison doors, the jailer assumed there was an empty jail. He knew his life would be taken because of the Roman law about escaped prisoners. He became suicidal. But out of the darkness of the prison there came the voice of Paul, "Don't harm yourself. We're all here!"

Alarmed at the earthquake, amazed that the prisoners were still there, confounded by the calmness of Paul and Silas, and overwhelmed at the proof of the presence of God, the trembling jailer fell down on his knees before Paul and Silas (vs. 29). Though he had probably supervised the scourging of Paul and Silas, deep in his heart he knew that they must be in the favor of God. He took them out of their cell and asked, "What must I do to be saved?" (vs. 30).

In the urgency of the moment, the searching question demanded a clear, definite answer. "Believe in the Lord Jesus . . ." (vs. 31). This is *the* answer, both for the jailer and for all of humanity! It is the answer that provides immediate peace, and assurance of the future.

"And your household." This same salvation was equally available to his family (see Lk. 19:9). They could call upon the same Lord for salvation. The jailer was reminded that they also needed salvation, and he was presented with the assurance that they could unite with him in the peace and joy of redeeming mercy. Old and young alike were instructed in the claims of Christ.

What a remarkable testimony to the life changing power of the Gospel! This very jailer a few hours earlier had thrust them into the inner prison and locked them in the stocks. He had shown no compassion toward their ripped and bloody backs. But no sooner was he converted than he was filled with compassion. He saw their suffering. He pitied them, and hurried to minister to their wounds. He fed them with all kinds of food.

He also rejoiced. This was the effect of believing. He was free from danger and alarm; he had evidence that his sins were forgiven and that he was now a friend of God. The ugly and alarming scenes of the night had passed away; the prisoners were safe; and faith, with its peace and pardon, had come to him and his family. What a change was produced in one night! What a difference between the time Paul and Silas were thrust into prison and when they were brought out and received as honored guests at the very table of the jailer!

With the foundation of two households and the healing of the demon-possessed girl, the church of Philippi was well on its way. Each person had experienced the love of God in a profound way. Each one's life had been changed forever.

Reach Out to Others

How many times do we stand by and do nothing while a neighbor's heart is breaking? A divorce, a death in the family, a mortgage foreclosure comes, and we say things like, "Oh, I didn't know you were having problems" or "Oh, I'm so sorry."

It's easy to sit back and do nothing when a problem is staring us in the face. But Paul and Silas didn't sit back—they took action! They saw the jailer's plight, the look of anguish in his eyes, and traded their freedom for his. This took initiative. It took compassion. Do we have this kind of feeling for our circle of friends?

Why not explore ways to get close to people who are in the midst of crisis—without stepping on their toes? How about going to the troubled friend and giving her a hug? How about inviting the childless couple over for coffee and cake? How about letting the just-fired husband cry on your shoulder? It's not fancy theology, but it works.

When we begin to reach out to others in meaningful ways, the Gospel really takes hold. People then know what we mean when we say, "Believe in the Lord Jesus."

For Discussion

1. List some methods of evangelism we can learn from studying Paul's encounter with Lydia.

2. Why didn't Paul and Silas try to escape when the prison doors were flung open?

3. What Christlike quality did Paul display in Acts 16:28?

4. How can you help others become aware of their spiritual need even if they feel no need for God?

5. In what area of life would you want to "throw Paul in jail" if he took away your source of income (or pleasure)?

6. Is there some uncharted "Macedonian" land in your own life? Where does the Gospel need to go that it hasn't already? Begin with yourself. What areas of your own life need a breakthrough—a fresh infusion of the power of the Gospel?

Window on the Word

Deliverance

A little boy once climbed to the top of a big barn. He was having a wonderful time up there, looking down at everything below. Suddenly, he slipped. He could see that he was going to be hurt if he fell on the rocky ground below, so he prayed, "Dear God, don't let me fall. Please don't let me fall on those rocks!" Just then, his pants caught on a nail that was sticking out from the roof. The nail stopped his fall. The little boy looked up and said, "Never mind, God. I got hung on a nail."

Many people have a similar view of God's presence in their lives. The "nail" just happened to be there, so they don't need God. What's wrong with this kind of reasoning?

2

An Apostle's Prayer

Truth to Apply: I have the promise of blessing as I join in partnership with others to proclaim the Gospel through word and deed.

Key Verse: And this is my prayer: that your love may abound more and more in knowledge and depth of insight (Phil. 1:9).

The finance committee sat around the table in the kitchen next to the fellowship hall and discussed next year's budget for the church. The item of mission giving was raised, and, stirring in his seat, one man blustered forth that not too much money should be sent out of the church; "It's not good business!"

Was the man right, or badly mistaken? Why?

Part of the Philippians' "partnership" (vs. 5) with Paul was their giving of money toward the spread of the Gospel in faraway lands.

Paul's deep affection for the Philippian church is evident in the first verses of this epistle. His prayer for them is one of thanksgiving, applicable to all Christians. He also makes certain requests on their behalf: for their continued partnership in spreading the Gospel; for their encouragement in knowing that God is constantly at work in their lives; for a growing love in discernment; and for lives filled with the fruits of righteousness.

Light on the Text

1:1 Although Paul and Timothy are mentioned together here in the greeting, it is Paul who is writing the letter. Whenever Timothy is mentioned throughout the epistle, he is referred to in the third person.

This is a letter to all the Christians at Philippi. The interesting word, however, is "with." Paul includes the leadership of the church, but only after recognizing them as part of the church. As Alec Motyer (*Philippians Studies*) states, "It means that leaders see themselves first as members of the body, and only then as ministers . . . the leadership of those who are content to stand among the saints as those who serve."

1:2 Both grace and peace are bestowed upon the Philippian Christians. Grace always comes before peace, for grace enables peace. Motyer again points out, ". . . God is always taking the initiative to act on behalf of His people and to keep them in possession of those blessings which He purchased for them with the blood of His Son."

1:3, 4   Christians need to be thankful for other Christians. This is a mark of spiritual maturity. Whenever Paul's thoughts turned to the Philippians, he was thankful to God, the Author of their faith and work.

1:4   Paul's thankfulness is justified, in light of what he remembers in his intercessory prayers for them. Here he sets the apostolic example of intercessory prayer for all believers.

1:5   Paul viewed the Philippians as partners with him in his missionary endeavors. All believers need to work together and engage in mutual support of each other to bring Christ's Good News to people around them.

"From the first day" perhaps suggests the incident of the convert Lydia's opening of her home to the missionaries (Acts 16:14, 15). This happened on the Sabbath—a few days after the evangelists arrived in the city. Through her hospitality, which helped in getting out the Good News, Lydia was "a partner in the Gospel."

1:6   Paul was "confident" that the Philippians would continue to be generous in the cause of spreading the Gospel, right up to the time of the Lord's return. ". . . it is God's doing from beginning to end: He inaugurates and He completes" (J. B. Lightfoot, *St. Paul's Epistle to the Philippians*). The concerned spirit of these Christians was due to God working in them "a good work."

1:7   "Defending and confirming the gospel . . ." These are legal terms denoting Paul's appearance before the court in Rome. Whether in prison ("in chains") or putting forth Christ's case before the court, Paul knew the Philippians were sharing with him in God's grace.

"Grace" denotes God's moving toward us and shedding upon us His unmerited favor, reconciling us to Himself, saving us. God also sheds His favor upon His people by supplying their needs, and by allowing them to serve Him. As converted persons, Paul and the Philippians shared the privilege of proclaiming the Gospel, and were empowered by God for this task; in this way they all partook of divine grace. "If it is a privilege to preach

Christ, it is not less a privilege to suffer for Him" (Lightfoot).

1:8   God alone can testify to the intensity Paul feels in his love for them through Jesus. As an apostle, Paul loves them ". . . with that tender concern which Christ Himself has and has shown to precious souls" (Matthew Henry).

1:9-11   Paul prayed that the love of the Philippians might overflow in "knowledge" and "insight." The first word denotes spiritual knowledge: knowing God and His truth; the second, moral perception. The one who loves must also do what's right!

Possessing a deeper experiential knowledge of God, along with moral discrimination, enables one to "discern what is best." These are the things that really matter in life; the highest and best.

One who chooses the best in life is "pure" and does not cause others to stumble. Through the work of Jesus Christ within, such a person leads an upright life, "filled with the fruit of righteousness." This kind of living brings glory and praise to God.

CHARACTERISTICS OF GOSPEL PARTNERS

They have a growing relationship with Christ.

They are missionary minded.

They love other Christians.

They are dependent upon God.

They pray for others.

They are faithful stewards of God's gifts.

For Discussion

1. Think of a person or group toward whom you feel close spiritual affection, as did Paul. How would your prayer differ from Paul's?

2. If Paul is truly our model (see Phil. 3:17), what can we learn from him about our relationships?

3. In this passage, what gives the believer encouragement and assurance? Realistically, how does this provide assurance in your own life right now?

4. If you were part of the Philippian church, how would Paul's intercessory prayer affect you? Why? Would your intercessory prayer affect someone else the same way?

Window on the Word

Selfishness: The Opposite of Teamwork

Speaking of selfishness among ministerial students, former businessman Keith Miller wrote: "When we got to the school I sensed that for me there was something terribly wrong at divinity school. Some of these young men seemed more full of themselves than had the men at the [secular] fraternity to which I belonged. There seemed to he an intellectual competitiveness that was very keen and somehow unloving" (*A Taste of New Wine*).

Concerning such selfishness F. E. Marsh stated: "Self-seeking, like the cuckoo laying its eggs in the other bird's nest, cares not what inconvenience others may have, so long as its own interests are served" (*The Spiritual Life*).

In contrast to these examples, true teamwork brings great satisfaction and accomplishment to all involved. The goal of all Christians should be the formation of a partnership in the gospel that transcends personal pride and comfort.

3

True Commitment

Truth to Apply: Christ gives meaning to all of my life, even when circumstances seem to be working against me, or when death itself is imminent.

Key Verse: For to me, to live is Christ and to die is gain (Phil. 1:21).

How ought a Christian to think about dying? Most of us like to avoid this question, as if ignoring it can keep us from facing the reality of our death.

Newsweek (May 1, 1978) published a special feature, "Living with the Dying." In it, the writer observed, "The American taboo against death has been so ingrained that the living have difficulty perceiving that the dying are people too. 'Americans have lately learned to humanize the poor, minorities, and other outsiders,' said psychologist David Gutmann of Northwestern University Medical School. 'Now we are realizing that the dying are the most dehumanized group of all.' "

What difference does faith in Christ make in the way we regard death and dying? When the doctor says, "I am sorry but . . ." When the angel of death hovers close to a dear one? When the inevitability of death can no longer be escaped?

Background/Overview: *Philippians 1:12-26*

Toward the end of his life, Paul was imprisoned. He realized that death might be on the way. To the Christians in Philippi, whom he deeply loved, Paul declared, "To die is gain!"

One prominent theme in chapter 1 is Paul's desire that in both his living and dying he would glorify Christ. As background for this important teaching, consider the violent death of Stephen, the first Christian martyr. Acts 6:1-8 introduces us to Stephen, describing him as "a man full of faith and of the Holy Spirit" who "did great wonders and miraculous signs among the people." The church in Jerusalem chose him, along with six other men, to "wait on tables" so that the apostles could give themselves "to prayer and the ministry of the word."

Stephen made a strong witness for Jesus Christ as he conducted routine church business. Therefore, the Jewish leaders soon became hostile toward him. Their confrontation with Stephen, reported in Acts 7, climaxed with Stephen's being stoned while a zealous young Pharisee named Saul watched over the garments of the executioners. Thus Saul, who later became known as Paul, the great apostle of Jesus Christ, saw Stephen glorify Christ in dying.

"While they were stoning him, Stephen prayed, 'Lord Jesus, receive my spirit.' Then he fell on his knees and cried out, 'Lord, do not hold this sin against them.' When he had said this, he fell asleep. And Saul was there, giving approval to his death" (Acts 7:59—8:1). This incident must have impressed Saul deeply and prepared him for his conversion to Christ.

Stephen glorified Christ by following His example. From the cross, Jesus had said, "Father, into your hands I commit my spirit" (Lk. 23:46). Stephen, as he was being stoned, prayed, "Lord Jesus, receive my spirit." Even more striking is the parallel between Stephen's forgiving of his murderers and Jesus' words, "Father, forgive them, for they do not know what they are doing" (Lk. 23:34).

As for Paul, he accepts all kinds of trials if it means the spread of the Gospel. In Caesar's palace that has indeed happened. Paul's firm commitment is to the cause of Christ, whether in life or in the face of death.

Light on the Text

1:12   Paul reinforces his own statement. Not only does he want the Philippians to know about his condition, but he also *says* he wants them to know. This seems to imply that Paul wants them to understand how he views his own condition: not negatively, but positively, through Christ.

1:13   It is important to realize *who* understood. The Praetorian Guard was very important in Rome. It comprised Caesar's personal guards as well as the bodyguards of prisoners awaiting trial by Caesar. It is also important *what* the Praetorian Guard understood—that Paul was in chains for Christ. While all suffering is traumatic, it is worse to have others misunderstand *why* you suffer. To be understood clearly is a blessing. In this case, everyone, especially those of "rank," clearly understood why Paul was suffering.

1:14   The effects of Paul's chains, along with the bold witness and furthering of the Gospel, encouraged many other Christians to "speak the word of God." In this way, the Gospel would go even further. Such was the love of the early Christians for the Good News.

1:15-17   Paul states the motives of those who were preaching:

envy and rivalry	goodwill
selfish ambition	love
not sincerely	

The properly motivated preachers were seeking to proclaim the Gospel with sincerity. On the other hand, those with less-than-pure motives sought to irritate Paul while he was imprisoned. They ". . . proclaim Christ from headstrong partisanship and with impure motives, having no other aim than to render my bonds more galling" (Lightfoot). While we are not shown the reason for such opposition, we do see how Paul handles it.

1:18 Paul continues to be single-minded in his devotion to the cause of Christ. If anything furthers that cause, then it's acceptable. Although some motives are less than pure, "Christ is preached." Because Paul's goal is being reached, because the cause is being furthered, Paul can rejoice.

1:19 Paul is not referring to his personal safety. His personal salvation is assured whether he lives or dies. This salvation will develop "the spiritual life in the Apostle, will be a pathway to the glories of Heaven" (Lightfoot). Some see Paul's use of the word as referring to his deliverance from prison.

To overcome these difficulties, Paul counts on the intercessory prayer of fellow Christians and on the Holy Spirit to provide wisdom and power. Prayers and the Holy Spirit will turn Paul's circumstance to good.

1:20, 21 Paul deeply desires that every aspect of his life—his preaching, his teaching, the way he supports himself, his relationships with others, even his dying—will bring glory to Jesus Christ. Since his confidence is in Christ, he contrasts what he hopes will not happen (being ashamed) with what he expects will happen (having enough courage to face his future: either life or death).

Paul wants to be bold. Holy boldness is indispensable for those who would serve Christ, "For God did not give us a spirit of timidity, but a spirit of power, of love and of self-discipline" (II Tim. 1:7). The life of Paul, as recorded in Acts and his letters, reflects the boldness of Jesus, who often confronted the Jewish authorities, speaking bluntly against them when they perverted God's truth.

1:21 Because the central purpose of Paul's life is to serve and exalt Christ, dying will be gain. Death will usher him into Christ's glorious presence.

This points ". . . to the alluring fact that the serving disciple, who has an ever-growing communion with

Christ while alive, will have an even richer communion when death has shifted the scene, without altering the continuity of his service" (Paul Rees).

The most important thing to Paul is that Jesus Christ be glorified. In part, this means:

(1) that He be given full and proper credit;

(2) that He be strongly emphasized as the center of reality;

(3) that He be praised as the only giver of salvation, the only way by which people can know the Heavenly Father;

(4) that His teachings be explained and understood, and that they be put into practice in the life of each believer.

1:25   Paul shows the secret of Christlike leadership: putting the welfare of others ahead of one's personal desires.

Paul wants very much to die and go to be with Christ, but he also sees the value of continuing in this present life, serving the churches and preaching the Gospel. He is willing to set aside his first desire—to be with Christ—in order to continue the hard work of preaching the Gospel and supervising new churches. God has called Paul to take His Word to the Gentiles (Acts 9:15). Therefore, Paul puts this task ahead of his personal wishes.

Paul's preference rests in his understanding that a Christian's first responsibility, always, is to do the will of God. That is why he calls himself one of the "servants" of Jesus Christ (Phil. 1:1). To be a servant means to follow orders. God has ordered Paul to do the work of proclaiming Christ and encouraging the growth of Christian congregations.

For Discussion

1. How does Paul view his trying circumstances? How do you? What does this mean for you on Monday morning and the rest of the week?

2. What were the effects of Paul's suffering?

3. What was the "single" success factor in Paul's motivation? What were the results of this success?

4. From this passage, list the distinctive marks of a Christian leader.

5. What would Paul have answered if asked, "What is the meaning of life?"

Window on the Word

Paul's Holy Boldness

In its nearly 2,000 years, the Church of Jesus Christ has had no bolder leader than Paul. Soon after his conversion, Paul went to Jerusalem. There he "talked and debated with the Grecian Jews, but they tried to kill him" (Acts 9:29).

In Antioch of Pisidia, Paul's straightforward proclamation of Jesus as the Christ led to trouble. Hostile Jews "incited the God-fearing women of high standing and the leading men of the city. They stirred up persecution against Paul and Barnabas, and expelled them from their region" (Acts 13:50). Acts records many similar responses to Paul's message.

At the council in Jerusalem, Paul stood up against those who wanted to require circumcision as well as faith in Christ for salvation. To contend with top church leaders at this council took great courage. At stake was the basic principle that we are saved by faith in Christ alone (see Acts 15).

These are several examples of the boldness God gave Paul. Without divine empowerment, Paul would not have been able to accomplish what the Lord had chosen him to do. When God calls a Christian to serve Him, He provides the necessary power, courage, and strength.

4

Stand Firm!

Truth to Apply: Being called to suffer for Christ's sake, I find comfort through fellowship with other believers. This comfort provides motivation for perseverance, and a common bond for unity in the faith.

Key Verse: For it has been granted to you on behalf of Christ not only to believe on him, but also to suffer for him (Phil. 1:29).

In her book of devotions, *Each New Day,* Corrie ten Boom writes, "Jesus said, 'Occupy till I come.' Do you think you have no opportunity to do this?

"I met a woman in Russia who had multiple sclerosis. Her feet and hands were paralyzed except for one finger. With that one finger she typed out Bible texts and inspirational books.

"This paralyzed woman's husband bound her typewritten messages together into books which then went from one person to another. She did this work until the day she died. She is now with the Lord. How happy she is! And I am sure that she has heard from many there who have read her literature, 'It was you who invited me here.'

"Do not say you are not healthy or strong enough— you have more than one finger to use for God's work!"

Suffering for Christ can sound somewhat romantic— especially if others know about it. But what about those who suffer in silence; and no one ever knows?

Paul urges the Christians at Philippi to persevere in believing and living out the Gospel. Paul Rees observes, "Philippi was a Roman colony, with its citizens enjoying the same status, the same prestige, as if they lived in Rome. . . . The apostle . . . is saying, 'You profess to be citizens of Christ's commonwealth. Very well, then let the way you live be as weighty as the strong words with which you make this high profession.' "

Since all Christians must answer "Yes!" to each of Paul's "if you have any" appeals ("Yes, there is consolation in Christ; Yes, there is comfort in love," etc.), he can draw his readers to an affirmation of their common ground. He challenges them to be consistently Christian in their treatment of others.

Light on the Text

1:27, 28 Like many of the early Christian churches, the one at Philippi was subject to persecution both from Jews who rejected the Christian claim that Jesus of Nazareth is the Messiah and from pagans who objected to the Gospel's repudiation of their life-styles. In spite of such hostility, Paul calls the Christians not to be "frightened in any way."

Steadfastness in the face of opposition comes, first, from standing together as a church, united in the Spirit of Jesus. Christians have solidarity, believing that "in all these things we are more than conquerors through him who loved us" (Rom. 8:37). Such faith enables them to stand firm.

Also, when Christians stand firm, they act as an omen for the nonbeliever. Motyer concurs: "It was the first ploy of the tempter to deny a God of judgement, and human eyes remain sealed to this conviction until they are opened by a true spiritual conviction. . . . Here indeed is conviction of sin: a person gripped by the awfulness of eternal loss. It arises from seeing a church standing for Christ, standing for eternal things, enduring worldly loss and disrepute for the greater riches found in the Spirit."

1:29, 30 ". . . their experience of the hostility of the world and of the ability to stand against it is one of the hallmarks of apostolic Christianity. The life worthy of the Gospel of Christ could not be a sheltered experience for them any more than for him" (Motyer). (See Romans 8:16, 17.)

2:1 This verse suggests a sense of urgency. Paul lays the groundwork for his appeal to Christian unity by calling Christ's followers to remember:

the consolation offered by Christ;

the comfort brought by the love of God and fellow Christians;

the comradeship in the Holy Spirit;

the tenderness and compassion they had experienced.

Instead of harboring selfishness, Christians are to cultivate empathy. They are to be like Oliver Goldsmith, of whom it was said, "He gave away his life in handfuls."

Paul uses a certain leverage in order to build empathy in his readers. He appeals to their own enriching Christian experience in the four clauses of verse 1. He is saying in effect, "If these things have been true of you, and you know they have, then . . . ."

The last of the four clauses in verse 1 of the King James Version (KJV) is rendered by the inelegant "bowels and mercies." Physiologically speaking, the word translated "bowels" referred not to the intestines but to the viscera (i.e., heart, lungs, and liver region). Ancient Greeks realized that when they were moved emotionally, they felt it in this region of their bodies. Today we might say, "at gut level." In other words, the apostle is appealing to their deepest feelings.

2:2 Paul asks the Philippians to make him happy, to "make my joy complete." How? By showing a like-mindedness centered in Christ and His Gospel. A statement in John's final letter echoes this sentiment: "I have no greater joy than to hear that my children are walking in the truth" (III Jn. 4). No joy can match seeing one's spiritual children living out the deeper implications of their faith.

"Being one in spirit and purpose." As Christians, Motyer says, we are to be ". . . literally . . . 'like-souled.' The 'soul' is the 'real person' and particularly his affections and will. If we allow the word 'love' to cover the emotional aspect of the unity we are to enjoy, then . . . Paul's vision of unity includes mind, emotions, and will." F. E. Marsh wrote, "There is not uniformity in the strings of a violin, nor unanimity of sound as the player draws his bow across them, but there is unity of spirit in the harmony produced by the skilled musician."

In order to have unity there must be unselfishness. Harmony is only achieved through humility. This is why verse 3 follows on the heels of verse 2 in Paul's plea for unity. He urges: Don't let disunity stem from personal selfishness.

2:3, 4 Paul's instructions in verses 3 and 4 are based on the attitudes of Jesus. In all things He pointed to His Heavenly Father as the ultimate in truth, wisdom, and power. His humility can be seen in His willingness to talk with and show concern for ordinary people. By washing the disciples' feet, He set an example of self-sacrificing service.

Imitating the Humility of Christ

The idea of Jesus Christ as servant is central to the first half of Philippians 2. Two of Scripture's most important passages on this theme are Isaiah 53 and John 13. You might want to take time now to read these passages carefully. Together, they provide a deep understanding of the servanthood of our Lord Jesus Christ and the pattern He has set for His disciples to follow.

Isaiah 53: The outstanding characteristic of this great section of the Bible is that service is rendered by means of the servant's suffering because God has chosen this way of redeeming His lost creation.

It is important to see that this passage is predictive. Though there is a legitimate historical reference to the nation of Israel, these eternal truths were lived out by Jesus on the cross. Some commentators say it does not really refer to Jesus Christ. Yet there is no solid reason to doubt an interpretation held by believers for many centuries.

John 13: The custom of Jesus' time was for guests at a banquet to have their feet washed by a servant of the host. Foot washing was a comfort extended as a sign of gracious hospitality, for the roads were hot and dusty, and the sandals worn in those days made feet hot and dusty, too.

Deliberately, our Lord took upon Himself the task normally given to the lowest of servants. No wonder Peter was shocked! Yet Jesus intended the foot washing to be a dramatic reversal of roles to contrast the standards of God's Kingdom with those of the world. He wanted to show that in God's Kingdom the greatest is the servant of all. Thus He completely upset the notion that menial work is done only by those of low status, while important people do not undertake such lowly tasks.

Jesus also wanted to set an enduring example for His Church. If the Lord could stoop and wash the dirty feet of His disciples, how can Christians ever afterward fail to render humble service to one another? He said, "Now that I, your Lord and Teacher, have washed your feet, you also should wash one another's feet. I have set you an example that you should do as I have done for you" (Jn. 13:14, 15).

Unity in Philippi

Church unity can be achieved through unselfish humility—this is Paul's thesis in Philippians. In order to illustrate this idea, Paul enlists four examples of unselfish humility in Philippians 2:

Christ (2:5-11), who had every right to latch onto first claims at anything, but relinquished that right.

Paul (2:17), who poured out his life, just as the priests would pour out an Old Testament offering.

Timothy (2:19-23), who instinctively demonstrated an unselfish disposition.

Epaphroditus (2:25-30), who was so unselfish that his health was in critical condition on behalf of the Philippian Christians.

Thus, to "the leading city of that district"(Acts 16:12) of Macedonia (or northern Greece)—in fact, the first Christians upon European soil—Paul wrote to stave off further squabbles.

For Discussion

1. Why do Christians suffer for their faith? How do you suffer? Why can Christians count this suffering a privilege?

2. What promotes unity among Christians? What causes disunity?

3. What is the difference between suffering and suffering for Christ?

Window on the Word

Persistence Pays Off

It was graduation day at the University of Nebraska in Omaha. Lines of proud young adults filed across the platform to pick up their hard-earned degrees.

In the midst of this procession came 72-year-old Mary Brand. Proudly she claimed her sheepskin, a master's degree in social work. She earned it because she planned to work with older adults in a county memorial hospital.

Her presence, despite a 50-year age difference between her and most of the graduates, was a tribute to the perseverance of a woman who, when many of her friends had settled for restricted horizons, had dramatically broadened hers. Her determination to live a life of continuing usefulness overcame the inertia that might have prevented her from going back to school.

Her secret? Having a clear purpose and a high priority. A Christian's purpose is to live for Christ. This takes perseverance. Those radically committed to Him stand out as much as a 72-year-old woman in the line of young graduates at the University of Nebraska!

5
The Mind of Christle

Truth to Apply: Christ gave up the glory of Heaven on behalf of others. I am called to practice the same kind of humility and obedience in my own life.

Key Verse: Your attitude should be the same as that of Christ Jesus (Phil. 2:5).

John is a master craftsman. He makes beautiful furniture from walnut, maple, and oak. In his workshop he spends many creative hours, especially enjoying his work on the lathe.

First John carefully makes the pattern for a delicately curved table leg. Then he locks a block of wood in the lathe, turns on the power, and begins to fashion the furniture. He presses a sharp chisel against the wood as it rotates at a high rate of speed. There is an earsplitting whine. Chips shower into the air as the wood is shaped into measured curves and spindles.

Often John shuts off the lathe and lays the pattern against his work to measure its conformity. This checkup shows him how much more he needs to cut away before the table leg takes its final shape. "A good pattern carefully followed," John often says, "is the secret of quality work."

So it is for Christians. In Jesus Christ, God has provided the Perfect Pattern for every human life. In what practical ways can we stop working, and "check ourselves" against Him whose love is perfect?

Motyer writes, "This passage is virtually unique in the Bible. Four times over, in the Gospels, we find the history of the cross of Christ; time and again the epistles turn to their favorite theme, the meaning of the cross, the wonder of its effect, the remission of our sins. But rarely does Scripture open to us the thoughts and motives of the Son of God, as He contemplated the cross, and this is the specialty of these verses. We see the work of redemption as He saw it. We see the Cross through the eyes of the Crucified. We enter into the 'mind' of Christ.

"But we do well to remember that we are privileged to enter into the mind of Christ not for the satisfaction of our curiosity but for the reformation of our lives. Paul has called the Church to worthy living, issuing in steadfastness under fire, and depending on individuals with correct assessments of themselves and correct aims in living. 'What am I calling you to?' he cries. 'To this: let this mind be in you which was also in Christ.' The vital element in the Church on earth is the individual fashioned after the likeness of his Lord in an identity of mind, for it is out of the inner man that the rest of life flows."

Light on the Text

2:5-8 There are two giant steps here, indicated by:

(1) He "emptied himself" (a literal translation of vs. 7), and

(2) "He humbled himself" (vs. 8).

First, He stepped into life on our planet. Then He stooped to death on a cross.

It must be remembered that in expounding this passage Paul wasn't composing a treatise on theology, but rather illustrating what it meant to be unselfish.

Therefore, by the "attitude" of Christ (vs. 5) he is talking about a disposition, or outlook, of "being for others."

The NIV's use of "being in very nature God" for "form of God" (KJV) implies not the external unessentials (such as facial features), but the essential attributes.

This means that Christ had whatever is essential to being God, and was therefore God. As John 1:1 says, "In the beginning was the Word, and the Word was with God, and the Word was God." That "Word became flesh" (Jn. 1:14). The term "God" in the New Testament is generally used of God the Father, while passages like our present one use other language to say the same thing of Christ and the Holy Spirit.

The statement is so colossal that it's a little like seeing a redwood tree for the first time—it's so gigantic that one's mind can't take it in.

The word "being" means that Christ was God before He "made himself nothing" (vs. 7). He didn't become God when He was on earth, at His baptism, for instance. He already was God before the events of verses 7 and 8. "Being in very nature God" is an equivalent to John 1:1, when, at the beginning of Creation, Christ, as God, was already in existence.

At verse 6 the KJV says: "Who, being in the form of God, thought it not robbery to be equal with God." The NIV is much more understandable: "Who, being in very nature God, did not consider equality with God something to be grasped." The idea is that Jesus refused to view His glory in Heaven as such a highly prized possession that it could not be given up on our behalf. What love!

"In very nature God." Father, Son, and Spirit exist together in the Godhead. We speak of this as the Trinity. Exactly how the coequal members of the Trinity relate to each other we do not know. Yet Father, Son, and Spirit remain one while being distinctly separate. There has never been competition for superior status within the Godhead. The Son obeys the Father.

The first clause in this verse may be translated, "Although He [Christ] existed in the form of God . . . ," What is the "form of God"? Ralph Martin called it ". . . the key term of the entire hymn" (*Carmen Christi*). B. B. Warfield held that in Greek thought it referred to the precise group of qualities that gave something its essence. In other words, to have the form of God would be to possess the essential character of God. Hence, Hugh Michael translated it, "Though he was divine by nature . . . " (*The Epistle to the Philippians*).

The next clause ("did not consider equality with God something to be grasped") has caused rivers of ink to flow. The hitch lies in what is meant by "equal with God" in this verse. Many scholars hold that it means something different from what it means in John 5:18. In John it is obvious that the Jews stumbled on Jesus' claim to essential equality with God the Father.

Rather than referring to Jesus' essential equality with the Father (as Jn. 5:18 does), many hold that the expression here refers to Christ's living on an equal plane with God, to His possessing equal external status with the Father. In other words, Jesus could give up this external equality without surrendering His essential deity. Jesus' deity is neither diluted nor deleted by this "emptying" (RSV, vs.7) in coming to earth.

J. B. Lightfoot gave the sense of the passage as "He stripped Himself of the insignia of majesty." What Jesus surrendered was the glory He had with the Father "before the world began" (Jn. 17:5). Lightfoot translated, "Yet [He] did not regard it as a prize, and treasure to be clutched, and retained at all hazards." Paul's Greek word translated "robbery" (in the KJV) is found only here in the New Testament.

2:7   "But made himself nothing." This refers to His coming to earth as a baby in the manger, growing as a boy in Nazareth, and dying on Calvary.

Whereas the first Adam grabbed at the idea of being equal with God (Gen. 3:5), the last Adam (I Cor. 15:45) surrendered the equal plane of glory by taking to Himself the body of a Hebrew carpenter. Instead of clawing and scratching, grabbing and flaunting His glory, Jesus "emptied" (RSV) Himself. Probably this expression is to be taken metaphorically rather than strictly literally. In other words, it is an understood picture, like saying "I struck out today at the office." No one would assume that you had carried a baseball bat to work that day. Rather, it would be a pictorial way of expressing your feeling of failure on the job. For this reason, James O. Buswell II translated "He emptied

Himself" as "He expended Himself" (*Systematic Theology of the Christian Religion*).

Verses 7 and 8 describe the Incarnation, or enfleshment, of God in Jesus Christ. He came to earth and lived a human life, except that He did not sin (II Cor. 5:21). Dwelling among us, fully human yet at the same time fully God, Jesus Christ experienced even death, that last great enemy of humanity. That God came to earth as a human being to die for a lost world is the unique claim of Christianity. Incarnation is a sign of God's great love in identifying with us. Charles Wesley wrote these familiar words we sing each Christmas:

> Veiled in flesh the Godhead see,
> Hail th' incarnate Deity!
> Pleased as man with men to dwell,
> Jesus, our Immanuel [meaning, "God with us"].

Many hold that Philippians 2:7 is essentially the same as that act of God's Suffering Servant in Isaiah 53:12 ("he poured out his life unto death"). In Isaiah 53:12, "poured out" is not literal either, but is a figurative way of expressing Christ's self-giving.

In one of his hymns, Charles Wesley said that Christ "emptied Himself of all but love." If he was thinking of I John 4:16 ("God is love"), then he has supplied a poetic description of Christ's emptying—He didn't give up His God-ness.

Of *what* did Christ empty Himself? The answer might be: of that eternal glory indicated in John 17:5.

But there is still further explanation of Jesus' emptying in the context. Verse 7 may be translated: "He emptied Himself by taking a slave's form." It is as if Jesus subtracted by adding. As Augustine put it in his *Homilies on the Gospel of John*: "He emptied Himself not by losing what He was, but by taking to Him what He was not." William Hersey Davis said that Paul is not stressing the royal status Christ forsook, but the servant's role that He took (Carl F. H. Henry, ed., *Basic Christian Doctrines*).

How did Christ empty Himself? By becoming every bit a slave in His outlook.

Jesus came "in human likeness" (vs. 7). Elsewhere Paul says He was sent "in the likeness of sinful man" (Rom.

8:3). He was "found in appearance as a man" (Phil 2:8). The word "appearance" refers to what is external, in contrast to "nature" (vss. 6, 7), which refers to what is internal and essential.

2:8   Not only did Christ empty Himself, but (giant step 2) "he humbled himself" (vs. 8). This He did to the extreme extent of death by crucifixion. The Roman statesman Cicero had said: "To bind a Roman citizen is an outrage; to scourge him a crime; it almost seems parricide to put him to death; how shall I describe crucifixion? No adequate word can be found to represent so execrable an enormity" (Hugh Michael, *The Epistle to the Philippians*).

The other key word is "appearance" in verse 8. This is the outward aspect. We see here the distinctive shape of Christ's face, hands, feet as if we had lived in Jerusalem in those fateful days. But the crucial things about Him were His deity and humanity, both inner matters.

"In very nature God" (vs. 6) then, shows that Christ is deity. "Very nature of a servant" (vs. 7) shows Christ's humanness. "In human likeness" (vs. 7) means that He resembled humans (while being more than human). "In appearance as a man" means He was observed to be human in His normal outward, changeable features.

The word "humbled" was rarely used as a virtue by the Greeks, who were more concerned with courage, truthfulness, etc. Even today humility is associated with spinelessness. Yet what Christ did was scarcely spineless. Literally, "humbled himself" means "made himself lowly." In dying a convict's shameful death, the one He obeyed was, of course, God the Father.

For Discussion

1. In light of this passage, how can you prevent your mind from being filled with yourself? What, concretely, can you do?

2. Why do we sometimes feel Christ's lordship threatens, rather than strengthens, us? That is, why do we sometimes look at His will as second best? How does the passage speak to this problem?

3. What does it mean that Jesus "emptied himself" (vs. 7, RSV). What was the twofold result of Jesus' self-emptying?

4. Put yourself in the place of Christ after He added human nature to His divine nature and subordinated Himself to God the Father. What changes were there from His former position in Heaven? (Try to get a feel for the enormous change of circumstances He had to undergo. Think of His relation to the political power structure; the religious power structure; the physical world; tiredness and thirst; and other characteristics of humanity but not deity.)

Window on the Word

An Ancient Parable

Once upon a time, there lived a king who had power over all nations and peoples. His courts were of richest splendor; his tables were heavy with the finest food. Music, laughter, and gaiety floated from inside the castle, and it was always light. Clouds wrapped it in ethereal majesty. Travelers always stopped and looked at the castle for a long while, wishing they might know the king who had built the marvelous structure. But none were able to reach it.

In the cold of winter, the king's tailor entered the royal chambers with his latest samples for the king's wardrobe. The little man was proud of his accomplishments. He had selected the finest materials and woven them into the most beautiful garments that eyes had ever seen. They glittered like gold.

But the king was not pleased. He ordered his tailor out, vowing to make his own clothes. No one but the king knew what he wanted. The door to the throne room was shut and locked. Weeks passed, and from inside came the clacking of the loom. The royal court waited with anticipation to see what the king would make for himself. They knew they were bound to be blinded by the glory of it. Finally the awaited day arrived. The doors opened and the king appeared.

Everyone, especially the tailor, gasped in surprise and horror. His Majesty was dressed in the simplest, cheapest, most unkingly garments imaginable. He had the choice of the world's finest materials, but he had chosen to wear the clothes of a beggar.

"I am going into the valley," he said quietly.

6

God's Response And Ours

Truth to Apply: Through the example of Christ's exaltation, I am reminded that obedience comes before blessing.

Key Verse: Therefore God exalted him to the highest place and gave him the name that is above every name (Phil. 2:9).

There is a story about a rather creative social worker. It happened in a run-down tenement house where a really slovenly mother and father lived with their children. Their rooms were filthy, a real disgrace. The social worker had tried almost everything she could to get them to improve things, but nothing had worked. As a last resort, she went to a florist shop and bought the most spotless white lily she could find. She took it to the tenement, and without a word of explanation, she placed it on the dining room table, and left.

The lily simply sat there in its gleaming purity, speaking a silent judgment upon the rubble around it. The woman got the message, and she cleaned up the dining room. Then she cleaned the kitchen and bedrooms. When the social worker returned, she hardly recognized the apartment.

Isn't this a lot like the mission of Jesus? He came to earth, experienced all the temptations and trials we face, but He did it without sin. Thus He was exalted. When we take Him into our lives, His holiness and purity are such a shocking contrast to our sin-cluttered life-styles that we simply must make the changes necessary to provide Him with a proper dwelling place.

Can you testify to this in your own experience?

39

Background/Overview: *Philippians 2:9-11*

Because verses 5-11 should be taken as a whole unit, this final portion of the text would not be possible or understandable except for the verses preceding it. The honor accorded to Jesus Christ at the end of the age will result from His faithful obedience. That is why the connective word "therefore" needs to be emphasized. It is the hinge on which the final three verses hang.

Why is this so important? Because it is one of God's enduring principles that obedience comes before blessing. First we understand what God requires; then we act; finally God sends blessing.

Yet many Christians seek God's blessing without bothering to obey Him. "Skip the hard part," they say by their actions. "Don't bother me with obedience; just bless me real good!"

To seek God's blessing without obeying Him is like expecting to harvest a rich crop without first plowing the ground, sowing seed, cultivating, and fertilizing. Foolish? Of course—but no more so than a Christian who seeks blessing without obedience to God.

Jesus teaches us that "everyone who exalts himself will be humbled, and he who humbles himself will be exalted" (Lk. 14:11). Peter says, " 'God opposes the proud but gives grace to the humble.' Humble yourselves, therefore, under God's mighty hand, that he may lift you up in due time" (I Pet. 5:5, 6).

Often we take Jesus for granted. We give more attention to our building funds, budgets, and youth programs than we give to Him. But let us never forget that Jesus Christ must be put first in everything! For when we exalt other things, we fall into the deadly danger of subordinating the Savior.

Light on the Text

2:9   "Therefore" is always a critical word. It says that what follows is due to what has just been said. It indicates a direct cause-and-effect relationship between Christ's humiliation and His exaltation (see Lk. 14:11 and Jas. 4:10). It was because Christ made Himself of no reputation, became a man, and died on a cross that God then exalted Him (see I Pet. 5:6).

To capture this effect, Paul coined the verb (one word in Greek) "highly exalted." We might render it "superexalted." The word is found only here in the New Testament. Jesus was exalted above all celestial, terrestrial, and infernal powers.

The Father exalted the Son by giving Him "the name that is above every name" (vs. 9). What name is this? It is probably best understood as "Lord." This accords with verse 11 and with other passages, such as Acts 2:36.

"Name" probably is used in the sense of "honor, authority." Similarly today we speak of "name" brands, meaning "reliable" brands. By exalting Christ, God automatically gave Him a name above every name.

Paul Rees, in his commentary on Philippians, says, "The two huge honors that impress St. Paul as he surveys Christ's exalted state are (1) what God does in bestowing on Him a name and (2) what men do in blessing that name."

Rees explains that there are two different interpretations of "the name of Jesus." One understanding is that it means "dignity, fame and honour" rather than the specific title "Jesus," "Lord," or "Jehovah." A second school of interpretation is represented by the Presbyterian preacher Andrew Maclaren, whom Rees quotes: "'The simple personal name [Jesus] was given indeed with reference to His work, but had been borne by many a Jewish child before Mary called her child Jesus, and the fact that it is this common name which is exalted above every name, brings out still more strongly the thought already dwelt upon, that what is thus exalted is the manhood of our Lord.'"

2:10, 11   It is most important to note that these verses are a reflection of the sentiments of Isaiah 45:21-23. This Old Testament passage is unmistakably about God ("I am God," vs. 22). Nevertheless, Paul borrows these very statements about God from the Old Testament and ascribes them explicitly to Jesus.

41

Thus Paul puts his finger upon the pulse of the New Testament affirmation—that "Jesus Christ is Lord" (vs. 11). This is essential to salvation, for we must acknowledge that "Jesus is Lord" (Rom. 10:9).

The phrase "Jesus Christ is Lord" is a doctrinal statement, a confession, a declaration of the early church. Historically it is one of the earliest "statements of faith," the first step in formulating later, more extensive creeds.

Yet His lordship is not independent of the Father, for when we say, "Jesus Christ is Lord" we are aware that we are praising the Father's glory, too.

In response to this crystallized confession of the early Christian Church, C. T. Studd, the cricketer-turned-missionary, said, "If Jesus Christ be God and died for me, then no sacrifice can be too great for me to make for Him."

2:11 Isaiah 45:23 is quoted, and its spirit is clearly present here. "Every knee will bow . . . every tongue will swear." As Paul says in Colossians 1:18, "that in everything he might have the supremacy." What is right and just will one day be done. If people do not voluntarily respond to Christ as Lord now, they will on some future day.

As Motyer puts it, this confession will be ". . . a grudging acknowledgment wrested by overmastering divine power from lips still as unbelieving as they were through their whole earthly experience. All will submit, all will confess, but not all will be saved."

For Discussion

1. How did God the Father exalt Christ?

2. Explain why you feel it was appropriate for God to exalt Christ.

3. What do these verses teach about Jesus' eventual recognition by the world?

4. Describe what happens to you when you neglect the worship (exaltation) of God.

Window on the Word

Pay What You Want

In the town of Sanger, Texas, is a most unusual restaurant, The Fatted Calf.

"The food is good, the entertainment is stimulating, and the prices can't be beat," wrote a reporter in the *Lexington Leader*. "On top of that, an evening there is designed to soothe the soul."

Dr. Ron Thomas (who is both a doctor and a non-denominational minister), his wife, mother-in-law, and a host of volunteers serve the Lord while they serve fancy Texas-size steaks to customers who write their own checks.

The left side of the restaurant's menu reads, "We are here to serve you. However, there is no price on our service. So when you have finished your meal, put whatever you desire in the jar on your table. And if you cannot pay, please take what you need."

"Some patrons haven't paid a thing and some have taken money from the jar," says Thomas's mother-in-law, Wanda Ragsdale. "But generally, people pay what is fair. In fact, patrons often pay more than their share. We've found that people love to be trusted. So far, we've had no reason not to show trust. . . . It's a joy to see the faces of tourists who just happen in and find out they are in what we consider our house of worship."

And what kind of religious faith is it that offers 12-ounce sirloin strips for nothing?

"We're simply believers," Mrs. Ragsdale says. "We believe Christ is the Son of God and that He died for our sins. This is our way of demonstrating our faith that the Lord will take care of us."

There is no preaching during a meal at the Fatted Calf . . . but all of the music is religious in nature. Mrs. Ragsdale says her family eventually hopes to establish a ranch for wayward boys on the land that adjoins the restaurant.

This family dares to put into practice a radical faith. They believe God will provide for them and protect them as they follow Christ's example of serving others without counting the cost.

7

A Life of Obedience

Truth to Apply: Christian character development is a growth process performed by the Holy Spirit working within me. Christlike obedience is a key evidence of this growth.

Key Verse: For it is God who works in you to will and to act according to his good purpose (Phil. 2:13).

A visitor to South India dropped in at a Men's Fellowship where 20 national Christians were meeting for prayer and Bible study. Besides their group devotions, the men went regularly to nearby towns and villages to share the Gospel with their Hindu countrymen.

The guest asked, "As you engage in your evangelistic work, what objection to the Gospel do you meet most often?"

The most experienced man in the room replied, "The obstacle most often referred to is the inconsistent lives of the Christians." Others in the group nodded their assent. They had met the same difficulty.

In what ways are we, as Christians, "walking testimonials" to the validity of the Christian faith?

Following his great discourse in verses 5-11, Paul now seeks to immediately apply what he has taught. He is answering the question, "So what?"

Light on the Text

2:12   A second "therefore" appears here. (The first is in verse 9.) This provides Paul the leverage to launch into a discussion of appropriate action.

Merrill Tenney has observed that Philippi was founded by Philip, the father of Alexander the Great. It was a center for mining gold and silver. How appropriate, then, that Paul used a contemporary expression for the mining process. The writer Strabo used it with reference to silver mines in Spain. He indicated that the ore there should be "worked out." In other words, they should bring to the surface what was buried under the earth. We, too, must "work out" our salvation. We must take what has been implanted inside us by God and extract it for expression to others.

Certainly there is a time to "wait on God" in prayer for guidance and help. But if God has told us in the Bible to do something, and then we talk about "waiting on Him," we are simply talking when we should be doing. We are the ones who must "work out" our salvation.

2:13   We must work. But as we work, "it is God who works" within us. Paul illustrates this Biblical combination (both God's work and our human work) in Colossians 1:29. Over our rightly motivated work we may imagine the words painted: "God at work."

Imagine the privilege, as a believer, to know that almighty God is working *in me*: graciously helping me not only to *do* good, but also to *want* to do good.

2:14   While the emphasis up until now has been on the person's being, Paul now begins to emphasize the person's doing. It is not just *what* is done but *how* it's done: "without complaining or arguing." This implies not only a limit on outward behavior, but also an exhortation to deal with the attitudes producing such behavior: a spirit of jealousy or envy, unrealistic expectations, unfair comparisons.

2:15   Now the goal of our actions is presented: to become (implying a process) "blameless and pure, children of God without fault" in the context of a crooked and depraved generation (that is, the unbelieving world at large). Here Paul uses a vivid comparison. We are like stars in the universe. Who we are (and are becoming) shines out for all to see and admire. The point is to show the contrast. (See Matthew 5:16.)

Born to Grow

We are born to grow, but growth is not inevitable or automatic. There are laws that regulate growth. For example: If you want to grow physically, you must eat regularly; you must get plenty of rest; you must exercise. No one questions these laws; we accept them without argument.

But when it comes to spiritual growth, we often seem to feel that it should occur automatically. It seems that many Christians have a hard time accepting one of the basic principles of spiritual growth: Growth requires effort.

Try evaluating your own life in terms of spiritual growth. Below are eight areas providing the context for Christian growth, with some practical ways of applying them in daily life. What other ways would you add?

Area	*Ways of Growing Toward Maturity*
1. Having a goal	**Set goals for Bible study, prayer, etc.**
2. Earthly things	**Pray for new attitudes; make new commitments.**

47

3. Rejoicing	Develop habits of rejoicing even in bad circumstances; offer thankful prayers.
4. Truth	Tell the truth at home, at church, at work.
5. Integrity	Strive to be genuine and honorable.
6. Justice	Seek fairness in daily matters. Become informed about and involved in correcting some case of injustice.
7. Purity	Maintain pure thoughts, language, body habits.
8. Doing things that are admirable	Improve quality of leisure-time activities.

2:16 Note the exhortation: not only to grow, but also to hold fast to the Gospel they have come to understand. Matthew Henry states: "It is our duty not only to hold fast, but to hold forth the word of life; not only to hold it fast for our benefit but to hold it forth for the benefit of others; to hold it forth as the candlestick holds forth the candle, which makes it appear to advantage all around, or as the luminaries of the heavens, which shed their influence far and wide."

Paul's boasting "on the day of Christ" will be due to the Philippians' own actions borne out of right attitudes. This "boasting" will not be pride, but rather an indication of his desire to keep from working in futility: "that I did not run or labor for nothing." (See I Thess. 2:19, 20.)

2:17 Paul implies that it is not he who is offering, but rather God who is offering Paul's involvement and commitment in service as a sacrifice. It is a sacrifice upon the sacrifice of the Philippians.

"The Philippians are the priests; their faith (or their good works springing from their faith) is the sacrifice" (Lightfoot).

So then, even if Paul is a sacrifice upon a sacrifice, he "congratulates" the Philippians on their good works. Such dependence on God, along with selfless commitment to fellow believers, is a model for our own behavior.

2:18   In light of all Paul has stated in this section, the Philippians should be happy. Paul affirms their happiness. "It is the will of God that good Christians should be much in rejoicing . . . If the minister loves the people, and is willing to spend and be spent for their welfare, the people have reason to love the minister and to 'joy and rejoice with him' " (Matthew Henry).

Notice that they may rejoice both in the work *they* are doing and accomplishing ("like stars in the universe") and with Paul in the results of *his* labors with them. Another leadership quality of Paul's was his willingness to share his joys with those he led.

For Discussion

1. If salvation is a free gift, how are we to "work out our salvation"?

2. What can the Philippians do to fulfill Paul's prayer in verse 1:10?

3. Compare Hollywood "stars" and Christian "stars."

4. How do verses 2:12, 13 present a panoramic portrait of what happens in a believer's life?

5. How do verses 2:12, 13 reveal God's concern with the inner being of a believer as well as outward actions?

6. How is choosing poverty for the sake of others a Christlike quality?

49

Window on the Word

Comfort Exchanged for Service

People have always marveled at Albert Schweitzer, who forsook comfortable theological prestige to go live in the Congo; or Mother Theresa, who labored among the lepers and outcasts of India. It is human nature, say psychologists, to seek a stable environment: in other words, a setting in which to feel comfortable. This can reveal itself in the form of going to church on Sunday morning, returning to a dinner table loaded with rich food (and having to resort to Alka-Seltzer afterwards), and comfortably forgetting that anyone beyond my circle could possibly have any real crying needs.

Dolphus Weary, a black Christian, told of his temptation to get out of the poverty pocket where he had been raised. Dolphus had education and sports going for him. But instead of settling down in comfortable suburbia, he chose to go back to Mendenhall, Mississippi, to help establish a spiritual oasis: a health clinic, and proper schooling for the people he served. He chose to do this, knowing it had meant painful physical persecution for his predecessor, John Perkins.

8

Called to Serve

Truth to Apply: Two examples of Christian service provide me with guidelines for serving others."

Key Verses: He [Timothy] has served with me in the work of the gospel (Phil. 2:22b). He [Epaphroditus] almost died for the work of Christ (Phil. 2:30).

Early in 1971, Pakistani troops took action against those seeking independence for Bangladesh. In the midst of the resulting death and destruction stood dedicated Christian missionaries. In *Christ in Bangladesh,* James and Marti Hefley express great admiration for the courage of these Christians, who risked their lives to serve Christ. Here is one typical incident:

"A massacre had taken place at the nearby University of Dacca. Phil Parshall, Bill Barnett and Ed Welch drove through the deserted streets to the campus. A small band of angry students stopped their car and led them to a servants' compound. 'Look in each room,' a young Bengali requested. 'See what the brave Punjabis did!'

"In the first room they saw a mother crumpled in a corner, her lifeless arms entwining two dead children. The second room was empty but bloodstained. The third contained an obviously pregnant woman, dead, and covered with flies.

"The American consulate in Dacca advised the American Protestant mothers and children and other nonessential adults, both Protestant and Catholic, to leave on evacuation planes. If they stayed, their safety could not be guaranteed. "But few were willing to go."

Why? In the words of other missionaries the Hefleys interviewed: "If ever our Bengali friends needed us, they need us now."

Are there any "limits" to Christian service?

People who can handle responsibility in difficult situations are not produced overnight. Years of preparation precede their years of effective service. Even heredity and environment have a significant role to play in making them the right people in the right place at the right time.

Timothy was just such a person. He grew up in an environment ideal for someone who was to be Paul's troubleshooter among the largely Gentile congregations of Greece and Asia Minor. Long before his family came into contact with Paul, Timothy had become familiar with the Old Testament. His mother, Eunice, and his grandmother, Lois, had apparently read the Hebrew Scriptures to him from the time he was a child (II Tim. 3:15). Because of Eunice's marriage to a Gentile, however, Timothy grew up under the influence of two worlds of thought, the Jewish and the Greek.

When Paul arrived in the obscure little town of Lystra on his first missionary journey (c. A.D. 46-48), Lois, Eunice, and Timothy all appear to have committed their lives to Jesus as their Messiah. On Paul's second missionary journey (between A.D. 49-53), Timothy had developed sufficient leadership potential that Paul added him to help Silas (Silvanus) establish the house churches that already dotted Asia Minor.

Timothy's background in Judaism and Hellenistic paganism made him a useful emissary to Thessalonica (I Thess. 3:2) and, a few years later, Corinth (I Cor. 4:17). Much of the time, however, he spent with Paul on his preaching missions (II Cor. 1:19; Rom. 16:21). He also accompanied Paul and several other associates to Jerusalem with the collection (Acts 20:4), and to Ephesus (I Tim. 1:3), where he handled the problems of the church, and where he may have been imprisoned for a time (Heb. 13:23).

A Closer Look at Timothy

Acts 16:1-3. Timothy was not only a "disciple" (vs. 1) but also "well spoken of" (vs. 2) by Christians in his hometown and in the larger nearby city of Iconium to the north.

I Thessalonians 3:1-8. In the one to two years Timothy had spent as Paul's assistant, he had graduated from being a learner to being Paul's troubleshooter and co-laborer. Prophetically ordained by the laying on of the hands of Paul and the elders at Lystra (I Tim. 4:14; II Tim. 1:6), he appears to have spent several months, perhaps as much as a year, working with Silas in the Christian communities in Berea and especially Thessalonica (Acts 17:14, 15; 18:5; I Thess. 3:2). Timothy's role during that time was probably not an easy one.

Acts 18:5. When Timothy and Silas finally arrived in Corinth (Acts 18:5), Timothy's leadership role apparently underwent a shift. His experience as a troubleshooter in Thessalonica was excellent preparation for his new role as a colleague of Paul and Silas on the instructional staff of the "Corinthian Bible College" for the next year and a half.

I Corinthians 4:14-17. Timothy had by now been associated with Paul for perhaps seven years and was one of Paul's leading troubleshooters. Paul consistently used the word "son" to refer to Timothy as one he had led to faith in Jesus (see II Tim. 1:2).

Timothy had become a solid Christian leader. By the time he pulled up roots, leaving Lystra and "going west" with Paul, he was already well spoken of by the brethren (Acts 16:2). Before we can minister to our communities effectively, we need a similar report by the leaders of our own church.

Light on the Text

2:19   Paul wanted to hear good news about the Philippians. But Timothy was trained to look for the things that Paul valued in order that they both might have joy in what truly mattered: the Philippians' own joy and continued spiritual growth.

2:20   Timothy had his spiritual gifts almost as a birthright, as an instinct derived from his spiritual parentage. ". . . he inherited all the interests and affections of his spiritual father" (Lightfoot). Therefore his concern for the Philippians will be genuine.

2:21   Paul's general observation of the Church is that most everyone is self-centered rather than Christ-centered. How much has the Church changed in the last 2,000 years?

2:22   Paul uses the words "father" and "son," illustrating not only a spiritual heritage but also a close-knit relationship. The work they did together was work toward a common goal: the furtherance of the Gospel.

2:23, 24   In spite of his circumstances, Paul is hopeful. He does not state conditions as to the sending of Timothy. He simply wants to know how they are. Paul consistently has his hope "in the Lord." He never loses sight of God's sovereignty.

     Epaphroditus, although the same name (root) as Epaphras in Colossians and Philemon, is distinct to this epistle. Both were native to their respective locales (Philippi and Colosse). "The longer form of the name is always used of the Philippian delegate, the shorter of the Colossian teacher. The name, in fact, is so extremely common in both forms, that the coincidence affords no presumption of the identity of person" (Lightfoot).

2:25   Paul has a full, three-sided view of others:

"brother"	- personal
"fellow worker"	- social
"fellow soldier"	- spiritual

Lightfoot points out that ". . . the three words are arranged in an ascending scale; common sympathy, common work, common danger, and toil and suffering."

     In one verse, Paul provides feedback to the Philippians ("message received") and also affirms the character trait of trustworthiness in Epaphroditus.

2:26   Paul gives two reasons for sending the messenger back: Epaphroditus is both lonely and distressed for the Philippians. Both reasons show the psychological awareness and sensitivity of Paul and Epaphroditus. Paul is observing these symptoms in Epaphroditus, and Epaphroditus is sensitive to the feelings of the Philippians, even long distance!

2:27   True! Epaphroditus did almost die. God's double mercy was on both Paul and Epaphroditus. He spared Paul's "sorrow upon sorrow" by healing Epaphroditus. Note that here it was God, not Paul's ministry, which healed.

2:28   Paul draws the discussion to its conclusion. He wants Epaphroditus to return, both to increase the Philippians' joy, and to decrease Paul's sorrow. (Again, Paul shows his psychological awareness!) Paul wants the Philippians to recover their cheerfulness, which was affected by the news of Epaphroditus's illness.

2:29   Paul's instructions to the Philippians are: Welcome Epaphroditus "in the Lord" (affirming his relationship with Christ) with both gladness and honor. Respect him for the work he's done for the Lord.

2:30   Why? Because he risked his life providing what you couldn't give me. This showed the depth of Epaphroditus's service, and the consequent honor. These comments only underscore Paul's initial comments about Epaphroditus's service (vs. 25).

    Lightfoot points out: "It seems plain . . . that Epaphroditus's illness was the consequence not of persecution but of over-exertion." If there is a moral to this section, it would seem to be that burnout, although inefficient, troublesome, and downright dangerous, is, nonetheless, honorable in service to the Lord.

For Discussion

1. What did Paul see in Timothy?

2. What is wrong with giving new Christians leadership responsibilities before they have learned through experience the basic facts of the Christian faith?

3. Why are Christians sometimes reluctant to share their leadership responsibilities?

Window on the Word

Passages

In 1976, author Gail Sheehy wrote an interesting and important best seller called *Passages*. The book dealt with the predictable crises of adult life—pulling up roots in the late teens; the trying twenties; the more realistic thirties; and the period of mid-life crisis in the "deadline decade."

The passages through which Timothy's life went suggest parallels for our own lives. By heredity and background, Timothy was ideally suited to minister to his world in Christ's name. You might well reflect on how the Lord has uniquely prepared you to minister in specific ways in your own community.

Timothy's apprenticeship was an arduous one. There was a brief "honeymoon" phase when Paul, Silas, and Timothy made their way to the towns in southern Asia Minor (which Paul had visited earlier) and gave the Christians the decrees of the Jerusalem Council (Acts 16:4, 5).

But when Paul's Macedonian vision took them to Philippi, Thessalonica, and Berea, Timothy's learning included riots and possible jailing (Acts 16:1—17:15). Although you may not be able to relate to such an extreme apprenticeship, you may readily understand the trials of preparing for leadership.

The stage arrives when you are on your own. Likewise, Timothy was sent back to Thessalonica to encourage the Christians there to stand firm in their faith in Christ and not become discouraged in the face of both Jewish and Gentile persecution. Only after all these "passages" was Timothy ready to be a full-fledged Christian leader to whom Paul could delegate a lot of responsibility.

9
Righteousness From Above

Truth to Apply: I can know the joy that comes from having God's righteousness through faith in Christ.

Key Verse: And be found in him, not having a righteousness of my own that comes from the law, but that which is through faith in Christ—the righteousness that comes from God and is by faith (Phil. 3:9).

"About eleven years ago after I had finished preaching one Sunday night, I gave an invitation to all church members who were not converted to come forward and commit themselves to the Master. As the invitation began I noticed one of our deacons coming forward from the back of the sanctuary. If I had been asked at the time to make a list of the most dedicated deacons in our church . . . . I would have put him in first place. When he came to the front and I shook hands with him, I simply asked, 'Are you coming to dedicate your life anew to Christ?'

"He then astounded me; he replied, 'No, pastor, I am coming to accept Christ as my Saviour and Lord . . . . A few nights ago I began to examine my own life. I discovered that I am nothing but a hypocrite. I was serving God and the church as a Christian should, but in my own heart I had never had a real conversion experience. That night I knelt at the side of my bed, and I invited Jesus Christ into my heart as my Saviour and my Lord. I am coming tonight to make public confession of this.'

"I really learned a lesson out of this. I learned that only God and the individual really know what is on the inside" (Dr. Harold Fickett, Jr., *Hope for Your Church*).

Is it possible for a good church member to be outside the Kingdom? How?

Here, Paul was not defending himself in the eyes of the Jews as he frequently did, for there was no synagogue in Philippi.

Paul was writing to show that there is no human-originated inheritance of membership in Christ's Kingdom. Even his own splendid racial background and conformity to the Law of Moses were by themselves insufficient to enable him to do the work for which God had called him. This was one of his constant themes. To the Ephesians, he wrote: "For it is by grace you have been saved, through faith—and this not from yourselves, it is the gift of God" (Eph. 2:8).

Light on the Text

3:1   After making the parenthetical comments about Timothy and Epaphroditus, Paul continues: "To proceed, then, brethren . . . ." (Motyer).

Stating the goal of the believer, Paul says to "rejoice in the Lord." Although he's said the same thing before, it bears repeating. In fact, it acts as a "safeguard" for the Philippians, to protect them from error.

3:2   Paul then proceeds to describe that error by issuing a clear-cut warning: Beware!

"Those dogs": an insulting, derogatory word; not even human; animals.

"Those men who do evil": those who look to actions as a necessary component for salvation.

"Those mutilators of the flesh": those who look to circumcision as a necessary component for salvation.

Paul makes his point clear: It is a gross error to claim that more than the saving work of Christ is necessary for salvation.

3:3   Does one need to first become a Jew before becoming a
follower of Christ? At Jerusalem a "circumcision
coalition" was formed. Paul and his followers stood
against this group.

The account of the first church council is recorded in
Acts 15. Here Paul won the support of the church
leaders. Circumcision was dropped as a prerequisite for
being recognized as a member of the Christian
fellowship.

Although Paul won a victory at the council, the issue
continued to plague him. (Galatians and much of
Romans are both addressed to this issue.) The Judaizers
followed him from city to city, and finally, at Jerusalem,
succeeded in getting him imprisoned by charging him
with polluting the Temple— bringing in a nonproselyte
Greek (Acts 21). Perhaps the circumcision controversy
caused Paul to think about the whole of Jewish legalism.
He wanted to clarify his position concerning the primacy
of faith and the sacrificial death of Christ. In this sense
the circumcision controversy was not only the first but
also the most important controversy in church history.

In the context of verse 3, then, "the circumcision"
means "the people of God." Who are "we"? Paul lists
three distinctives.

1) The first, "who worship by the Spirit of God," harks
back to the Messiah's encounter with a Samaritan woman
at Jacob's well (Jn. 4). Christ explained to her, "God is
Spirit: and his worshipers must worship in spirit and in
truth." The externals, like place of worship or
circumcision, are nothing if the true desire of the heart
is not to adore God Himself.

2) The second distinctive is "who glory in Christ
Jesus." Perhaps "exult" might be a better word than
"rejoice." Believers "boast" of what Christ has
accomplished.

3) The third distinctive is really a negative way of
putting the second: believers have "no confidence in the
flesh." They do not trust their own achievements to
make themselves acceptable to God.

3:4, 5   Paul admits that he, too, could find things in his past to
hold up to God if that were what God wanted. If anyone
thinks he has impressive credentials, let that person

compare them with Paul's. Paul is not a convert from some pagan religion. He is truly a natural branch, blossoming from the stock of Israel, God's special people.

R. P. Martin says, "Within the national life of God's chosen people he claimed adherence to a special tribe, that of Benjamin. This tribe was regarded with particular esteem, in spite of its smallness ('little Benjamin', Ps. 68:27)."

Scholars suggest various reasons for the tribe's place of honor. Situated in the south, it may have resisted the encroachments of paganism from the north. It had the unique privilege of containing the Holy City and the Temple. It remained loyal to the house of David after the disruption of the monarchy, and earlier, in the field of battle, it had held the post of honor. Israel's first king was drawn from its ranks, and this king had the apostle's original Hebrew name. All of this must have contributed to Paul's special pride in his tribal association.

" 'A Hebrew of Hebrews' carries the meaning . . . 'the Hebrew son of Hebrew parents,' and informs us that the language in which he was reared and taught was the ancestral mother tongue of his race. Ability to speak the ancient languages (Hebrew and Aramaic) was a mark of faithfulness to the old culture, and commanded special attention, as we know from the scene in Acts 22:2 when Paul addressed the crowd in Aramaic" (R. P. Martin, *The Epistle of Paul to the Philippians*).

3:6   Paul the Pharisee had expressed his religious zeal when he persecuted those Jews who called Jesus the Messiah (see Acts 8:1, 3). He had felt that he possessed the kind of righteousness the written Law demanded. In this respect, he had appeared to be "faultless." It was in these credentials that Paul had once taken pride.

3:7, 8   Paul had many advantages by birth and training. Although a Jew, he was also a Roman citizen. This was an honor, and a source of many privileges not granted to others. In a world divided by class distinctions, he himself was considered a first-class citizen. This was why he had been brought to Rome for trial before Caesar.

Paul was a native of Tarsus. Natives of this university city were held in high esteem because of their access to learning. In addition, Paul had received special training under Gamaliel, a highly respected member of the Sanhedrin. Having studied under this man carried the same sort of prestige among Jews of Paul's day that having studied under Albert Einstein would have for a scholar today.

Beyond this, Paul belonged to the Pharisees. They were very legalistic with the Law and went to extremes in their interpretation of it. Like others of the group, Paul had, in his years as a rabbi, tried to squeeze joy and happiness from the Law while rejecting the new Gospel of Christ.

Before Paul met Christ on the Damascus Road (Acts 9), he saw salvation as a credit-debit account: could he produce a distinguished list of accomplishments that would assure God's acceptance of him? Given what he says in verses 5 and 6, he was sure he could. Meeting Jesus, however, made him see the uselessness of credentials. God has no use for a balance sheet when dealing with people's souls.

"Profit" may be understood as "assets" or "gain"; It came to this: on the way to Damascus he was still treasuring his assets as currency with God. When Christ revealed Himself, Paul's assets were shown to be what they had been all along: liabilities. Hence, he considered them "loss for the sake of Christ."

"What is more" is a strong introduction meaning an emphatic "in fact!" It ushers in Paul's assertion that all things humans consider religious currency are worthless when compared to the completely superior knowledge of Christ Jesus.

"Knowing" in this sense is not abstract, as in the phrase "textbook knowledge." The apostle did not simply exchange Judaic religious rules for Christian ones. The catalyst in his conversion was an encounter with the living Christ. Knowing Christ personally is worth more than any religious external he may have been proud of in the past.

In becoming a follower of Jesus, Paul relinquished the use of his credentials (which is why he is unwilling to mention them; compare II Cor. 11:16) and lost the respect of many of the Jewish authorities he had once worked with. ("I have lost all things.") But he saw these as of no more value than household refuse ("rubbish"). To "gain Christ" is, by definition, to lose everything else upon which one may pretend to rely—but the exchange is well worth it.

3:9   To "be found" means "to be known" by God and others as one who no longer trusts in the legal kind of righteousness he had before. Now, through Christ, he has the God-given righteousness by faith.

For Discussion

1. Why does Paul think it necessary to stop relying on his "credentials"? Why does he list them anyway?

2. What are some modern-day equivalents of "putting confidence in the flesh"?

3. Define "value" in terms of the world, yourself, Paul.

Window on the Word

God Has Chosen You!

In *The Little Prince* we meet a small boy and a talking rose. Despite the fact that this rose is very vain, and demanding, and entertains grandiose ideas of its own power, the prince comes to care for the flower.

In the course of time the little prince realizes why he loves the rose. It isn't because it is the most beautiful rose (for there are many just like it), and it surely isn't because the rose is kind to him. He loves it simply because it is so helpless.

It is a humbling—and exciting—realization to know that God loves us not because He is impressed by our talents or efforts or even our faith, but only because He has chosen to love us. (Ralph DiBiasio-Snyder, *The Quiet Hour*)

10

Paul's Example

Truth to Apply: Christian growth is an absolute necessity. In the life of Paul, I find a model for my attitude toward this growth.

Key Verse: I press on toward the goal to win the prize for which God has called me heavenward in Christ Jesus (Phil. 3:14).

Consider the life of Dr. David Livingstone, the 19th century Scottish explorer. On his last journey in Africa, he was determined to discover the source of the Nile. This discovery would accomplish two things. It would enable him to get the ear of the world so he could speak out against slavery—"the open sore of Africa." It would also open the dark continent to missionaries.

The world remembers the struggles he went through in order to accomplish this end. He had over 100 attacks of malaria. He lost his teeth, his baggage, and his money. Indeed, he became so ill he had to be carried much of the way. Finally the end came—he was found dead on his knees.

Livingstone never found the source of the Nile. His entire search was hundreds of miles too far to the south. Moreover, the source had already been discovered!

Nevertheless, Livingstone did see some movement toward the accomplishment of his goal: on the very day he died, England signed a treaty closing all of their African ports to slavery. The force that inspired the British government to do this was public opinion. A lonely, *totally committed* missionary, braving disease, poverty, and hostile natives had won the day.

What would a modern, totally committed Christian be like?

Background/Overview: *Philippians 3:10-16*

Although a prisoner, Paul had left behind him a remarkable trail of accomplishments. He had won many converts, founded churches, withstood the Judaizers, broadened the concept of Christianity, and had written immortal passages that were already inspiring the world. Yet he felt he was still reaching forward.

Some in the congregation apparently felt they had already "arrived." Paul lets them know that even he did not feel he had arrived.

Paul's spiritual goal was to be like Christ; but in his struggle to attain it, he was constantly bumping into his own humanity. He was quite candid about this. (See II Corinthians 4:7.) He realized that he could never be like Christ in his own power. Any righteousness he might attain would be through faith in Christ.

Light on the Text

3:10   The word "know" here has much more than just intellectual meaning. Paul wanted to know Christ until life was literally saturated with His personality! As in verse 8, "know" is experiential and personal. Knowing Christ more intimately means having within oneself the same force that raised Christ from the dead.

Paul did not suffer on a cross. But he experienced many pains similar to those known by Jesus: suffering the pain of loneliness and misunderstanding; witnessing cruelty; being beaten and abused. Yet through all of this Paul was enabled to write imperishable letters and build up churches, and he was ready to die with joy in his heart.

Pain causes some to be cynical and bitter. But Paul turned pain into blessing—just as solar cells turn the heat of the sun into electrical current.

3:11   Conformity to Christ's death is not necessarily crucifixion or martyrdom. Rather, Paul is thinking of death to sin, an act that allows Christ to shine through (II Cor. 4:10) and which frequently attracts the wrath of Satan. Paul means to participate "in the sufferings which Christ endured in his mortal life. . . . Being in Christ involves fellowship with Christ at all points—his obedient life, his spirit, his sufferings, his death, and his glory" (Vincent).

3:12 One of the great temptations in the Christian life is to become complacent—to settle down and become satisfied. Paul warns that this ought not be. He forthrightly states that he has not obtained full maturity. His admission shows the need for all Christians to continue growing.

Paul reveals the formula he has adopted in his own life and recommends it to others. He has renounced all that is negative in his past, all that would upset his hopes for the future. External legalistic religion, prior sins, and all encumbering allegiances, he has left behind. He now concentrates on reaching his goal.

Paul pictured the Christian life as a race. Like a runner, he determined not to carry anything unnecessary that might slow his speed. So he turned his attention away from his sinful past.

Paul may sound as though he now has the proper perspective on all things and only needs to await Christ's return. "Not so!" he says. "Full maturity is not yet mine. I still pursue it."

3:13 His description of the pursuit is stirring. The words "forgetting," "straining," and "press toward" create images of constant enthusiastic hard work, the work a runner does when he concentrates everything on winning. But this is not the work of a Pharisee making himself acceptable. This is the work of a sinner glorifying the God who forgave him.

3:14 As Christians we must have eyes only for the final goal. Like a runner, we keep our thoughts on winning the race. We set our eyes on the wire and determine to reach it. At the end of the way, there is a reward for the faithful and growing Christian. Probably the greatest prize of all will be the joy of sharing the victory our Lord has already won for us at Calvary. Then we will hear Him say, "Well done, my good and faithful servant."

The phrase "one thing I do" suggests the needed intensity. In the athletic competition of Paul's day, the prize was set at a point near the end of the course where all the runners could view it. This encouraged the competitors to strain every nerve and to put aside everything but their one objective.

His one consuming desire is to attain the resurrection in order to receive the prize. " 'The high calling of God in Christ Jesus' [KJV] does not denote [the prize's] content but rather that God's call has come to him that he might enter for and attain the prize" (Martin). What is the prize, then? Perhaps it is the Lord Jesus Himself. Perhaps it is the crown of life (I Cor. 9:25; II Tim. 14:8; Jas. 1:12). Perhaps it is the distribution of rewards to faithful believers (I Cor. 3:14; 9:24). Perhaps it is all these and more.

3:15   Paul is pleading for a unity of attitude and thought among Christians. Although some in the Philippian church already agree with his commitment to pressing on toward maturity, Paul wanted the entire Philippian church to present a solid testimony to the others.

"Mature." All who are mature in the faith should think in the way Paul has outlined in verses 1-14. He has tried to correct the Judaizing influence as well as to teach the Christian view. Then, speaking to anyone still confused on these points (or stubbornly adherent to false doctrine), he says, "God will make this clear to you" (*Today's English Version* [TEV]). Until He does, the believers should follow the basic truths Paul has taught them.

Every sincere Christian wants to achieve spiritual maturity—to become like Jesus Christ. The disciple strives toward that goal. It is the purpose for which Christ has laid hold of each of us. When the apostle Paul examined his own life, he found there was still much growing to do. He pressed on toward that day when all his hopes would be realized.

3:15,
16   Paul emphasizes that spiritual maturity is possible only when we strive for something better. There can be no

thought of already having arrived. Nonetheless, the apostle remains compassionate toward those who do not yet understand this. He believes God will lead them to see matters as he does. "Meanwhile, he says (in vs. 16) that until you have fuller light, be content to be open-minded and teachable, and guide your life by the light you have received" (R. P. Martin).

Paul, however, knew that all Christians had attained a certain level of maturity in at least some areas of their lives. In these areas we are to hold fast. There are many things even trained theologians do not understand. Yet they do not give up the things they do understand! We *do* have complete assurance about the power of the Word; the reality of salvation; the necessity of repentance; the assurance of the return of Christ; and God's absolute sovereignty.

For Discussion

1. In what ways can we share in Christ's sufferings?

2. Paul is very open about his process of growth. What is it like? What has it been like in your own life?

3. In verse 14, Paul identifies the Christian's goal as "to win the prize to which God has called me." What might this phrase refer to?

4. Share a definition of Christian maturity that is appropriate to your present life situation.

5. Are you more mature now than you were a year ago? How do you know?

Window on the Word

Run with Everything You've Got

After watching the new runner make the rounds of the track several times, the coach called him aside.

"Do you want to win when you run?" he asked.

"Of course I do. Why else would I be out here?"

"Well, you could be moving a lot faster."

"I could? My feet can't move any faster."

"Maybe not," said the coach, "but your arms could help you out by being used more effectively. Your legs could make better strides. Your head could hold itself up instead of hanging down. And you should lean into the tape at the finish instead of ending erect."

"In other words," said the young athlete, "I should run with everything I've got."

"Precisely. With everything you've got."

11
Realistic Christian Unity

Truth to Apply: I get perspective on Christian unity in light of those in error. I am called to help resolve disharmony within my own local church.

Key Verse: Agree with each other in the Lord (Phil. 4:2b).

A young American soldier was captured by a Japanese soldier during World War II. Ordering the American to walk ahead, the captor followed, holding a bayonet to the prisoner's back. As he was a Christian, the American soldier whistled a hymn to ease his fear. Soon the Japanese soldier began to whistle along with his prisoner.

Thinking he was hearing an echo, the American listened. Then the Japanese said to him as he came alongside, "I am a Christian, too. I learned several English hymns in a mission school." They stopped walking, had a time of fellowship together, then parted peaceably.

Can the Spirit of Christ really triumph over rivalry and hatred? How?

Paul warns the Philippians about the enemies of the cross of Christ. The power of Christ is their hope in overcoming problems both outside and within the church. In an atmosphere of love, Paul exhorts specific Philippians to dwell in unity. This exhortation is relevant for us today.

Light on the Text

3:17   Paul gives another exhortation to imitate him and others who live like him. He reminds them that in Christ they are members of the same family.

This verse is linked to the following one by the word "for."

3:18   Paul consciously repeats himself, stating, "I have often told you before and now say again . . ." Repetition shows the importance of the message. This importance is so intense that Paul is in tears. As Motyer points out, Paul ". . . taught the truth, but he was not a detached, disinterested teacher; he warned about error and wept over those who held it."

Paul was not a hardened intellectual without feeling, nor was he unduly emotional. He had true compassion for the lost, even the "enemies of the cross of Christ."

Who are these enemies? Lightfoot says that "'enemies of the Cross are both those who deny the efficacy of the Cross, substituting obedience to a formal code in its place; and those who refuse to conform to the cross, living a life of self-indulgence."

3:19-21   These verses provide a series of contrasts, illustrating the errors which have trapped so many. It is a study of spiritual degeneration ending in destruction; but it is also a study of spiritual hope ending in victory.

The threefold error of their ways, involving a progressively downward spiral, includes:

1. indulging themselves ("their god is their stomach");
2. twisting ideas of right and wrong ("their glory is in their shame");
3. thinking only about what they can get in this world ("their mind is on earthly things"). (See Rom. 16:17-19.)

Paul contrasts this with the Christian difference, a study in hope involving:

1. focusing on Christ ("eagerly await a Savior");
2. relying on His power ("the power that enables him to bring everything under his control");
3. knowing we have a promised future ("our citizenship is in heaven"). (See I Cor. 15:35-49.)

These points are summarized below:

	ERROR	CHRISTIAN
Focus	self	Christ
Morals	declining	renewing
Attitudes	earthly	heavenly

Beware of the False Teacher!

An obvious need in society and in today's church life is a sense of belonging. Our disjointed world creates a strong desire for fellowship, and many men and women satisfy this hunger by joining religious organizations. Unfortunately, some people opt for authority figures who offer simplistic answers to life's tough problems. Those who have difficulty making decisions or resolving conflicts, and those who lack positive structure in their lives, may develop an unhealthy dependency on leaders. Such individuals often are willing to trade self-determination for a sense of security—even if the security is only superficial.

Leaders sometimes exploit these dependencies and produce personality cults. Blind obedience may be demanded by the person in authority, and anyone who questions a teaching or practice may be considered to be "a tool of Satan."

In contrast, growing Christians, while appreciating the helpful insights provided by responsible pastors, teachers, and other leaders, evaluate all teachings in the light of the Scriptures, and never surrender the freedom to reject ideas that appear inconsistent with the Word of God.

4:1   Now Paul exhorts the Philippians on the basis of all he has said in the previous verses. First, he showers them with love and affection, calling the brethren "loved," "longed for," and "dear friends." Such sincere emphasis points to the apostle's depth of affection toward the Philippians. That he longed for them in the same way Epaphroditus (one of their kinsmen) longed for them (Phil. 2:26) shows how closely Paul identified with them.

That they are already Paul's joy is well established. They are also his crown. "When Paul thus uses these words, he has his mind fixed on the day of Christ and our gathering together with Him. . . . The crown can be equally that 'of victor or holiday-maker' " (Lightfoot). To Paul "it is a victory to see them accepted before the throne, and at the same time the proper garland of one who is banqueting with the King of Kings and His chosen guests" (Motyer).

Then, the Philippians are told what to do: stand firm. (See Ephesians 6:10.) "To 'stand fast in the Lord' is to stand fast in His strength, and by His grace; not trusting in ourselves, and disclaiming any sufficiency of our own" (Matthew Henry).

4:2   Two women (possibly deaconesses) are having a disagreement over an unidentified issue. Both of them are encouraged to "give up their differences and live at peace in the Lord" (Lightfoot). The responsibility for solving their conflict rests on both of them. Neither woman is singled out as being in error. And reconciliation is possible because they are both "in the Lord."

4:3   The women with the disagreement were not only of concern to Paul because of their problem with unity.

They had actually *labored with* Paul in spreading the Gospel. Therefore, he would know them and be particularly concerned for their welfare.

The exact identity of the "loyal yokefellow" is unknown. A faithful Christian close to Paul, possibly Epaphroditus, is being singled out for special and specific service: reconciliation. He is to be joined, however, by Clement and the rest of the church. Lightfoot says that the "apostle is anxious to engage ALL in the work of conciliation."

No Christian is at liberty to stand aloof from the needs of any other Christian. The very existence of the need is of itself a call to come to the rescue. Paul does not say to Euodia and Syntyche that they should ask the "loyal yokefellow" for his help. The command to him is to make the first move (uninvited, save by Paul). "If any of you would live up to your place and duty as Christians, take this yoke on you and help the women out of their tangled life" (Motyer).

Thus, the unity of a church is to be both the concern and responsibility of everyone within it. As Motyer again puts it, "The Church on earth is to be a replica of the ideal or heavenly. This is involved in the possession of heavenly 'citizenship.' . . . Thus it is against the nature of the Church, the community of the redeemed (Acts 20:28), to confess unity in Heaven and practice disunity on earth."

Paul seems to be asking: Given the great disparity we have with those in error outside the church, should differences be so large within the church?

For Discussion

1. What are some examples of modern spiritual degeneration?

2. What can we learn from Paul about the role of love in interpersonal relationships?

3. What does it mean to "stand firm" in today's world? Be specific.

4. What are some actions one can take to reduce conflict in the local church?

God's House Divided

Item 1: A rural church in the South, unable to afford a full-time pastor, asked two qualified lay preachers to take turns supplying the pulpit. For 20 years the men alternated Sundays and gave excellent sermons.

Over the years the attendance increased, and so did the offerings. The two men retired at about the same time, and both urged the church to call a full-time pastor. The congregation did so, and that's when the problem surfaced.

Members had developed a fierce loyalty to one or the other of the preachers. In fact, those who attended services when Mr. A spoke never came on Mr. B's Sundays and vice versa. Attachments to the individuals were so strong that neither group could support the new pastor. Charges and countercharges flew back and forth, destroying the church's witness. Eventually services were suspended, and the church disbanded.

Item 2: During the early days of radio, a dynamic pastor came to a church in the Midwest. By broadcasting services, the preacher attracted many curiosity seekers; some joined the church.

Although the work seemed to flourish, members of the church board were becoming apprehensive about the pastor's growing arrogance. He resisted their suggestions and seemed determined to make all decisions. More significantly, he was seizing control of various funds. In time, serious questions were raised about his use of contributions mailed in from listeners.

When matters came to a head, the pastor pulled out with scores of recent converts who insisted "their man" could do no wrong. The reputation of the church was tarnished, and bitter feelings infected the fellowship for 40 years.

A denominational executive who dealt with both situations said, "These churches never understood the roles of leaders and followers as taught in the New Testament. We must constantly hold before Christians what the Bible says about the nature and mission of the church."

12
Joy and Peace!

Truth to Apply: As I incorporate into my daily life the qualities of joy, thanksgiving, regular prayer, and right thinking, I come to know the peace of God.

Key Verse: And the peace of God, which transcends all understanding, will guard your hearts and your minds in Christ Jesus (Phil. 4:7).

Marshall Evans was like few people in First Church. It was when Stanley, his son, lay near death after a fall that the difference between Marshall and practically everyone else became most obvious. You could tell he was grieving for his boy, yet he was not anxious or edgy.

After Stanley recovered, someone asked Marshall how he was able to keep his composure. He answered in his simple, direct way: "I have learned how to be at peace. Although it was not always this way, I'm glad I discovered what few people seem to know. It isn't really a secret, of course. It's just prayer, the same thing we all have talked about but so rarely follow through on."

Marshall Evans apparently learned one of Christianity's not-so-secret secrets: how to have peace and joy regardless of circumstances.

How realistic is it to think that we can actually live such a life? What are some examples from your own experience?

In recent years people have been turning inward in search of personal peace. They have been willing to attend seminars, consult psychiatrists, try meditation, jog, practice yoga, change their diets, or do anything else to possess such peace. These methods have produced some success, but the peace they offer is not the peace of God. The reason: that peace is His, and only He can give it.

In this passage we are exhorted to be joyful, free from anxiety. We are to pray, and exhibit the finest of character traits in both our thoughts and deeds. Thus, we will have the peace of God.

Light on the Text

4:4 "Rejoice." The word suggests celebration after an important accomplishment, like a marriage or a victory. It pictures people who have forgotten themselves and their cares in the joy of the occasion. Indeed, long faces would be quite out of place.

"In the Lord" reveals the root of Christian joy. The Lord Himself, as Philippians 2 pointed out, humbled Himself and died for us. Therefore, He has been raised to ultimate prominence, and Christians share in His victory as they come to God through faith. It is as though Paul had written, "Rejoice in *who* the Lord is and *what* He has done."

According to Jeremiah, one should not boast on account of being wise, mighty, or rich, but because of the inestimable opportunity of knowing the living God (Jer. 9:23, 24). This same Old Testament prophet called the awaited Messiah "The Lord Our Righteousness" (Jer. 23:6). This is the touchstone of our faith: we have no righteousness except what He has gladly chosen to provide at great personal expense.

"Always" lets the Philippians know that in spite of their tribulations and Paul's imprisonment, rejoicing in the Lord is always appropriate. So emphatic is Paul that he repeats the statement.

4:5 "Let all men know your forbearance. . . ." (RSV).
Forbearance is ". . . the uncomplaining readiness to
accept others as they are and to submit oneself to their
demands" (Motyer). It is ". . . the opposite to a spirit of
contention and self-seeking" (Lightfoot). "Graciousness"
is a good modern equivalent.

"Evident to all" suggests that a believer should resist
the desire to retaliate after an attack. In this way he or
she can exhibit Christian forbearance.

This difficult instruction is sandwiched between
rejoicing in the Lord and the expectation of the Lord's
return. Implicit in the reminder is the knowledge that
God intends to give what is due to each person, thereby
underscoring the importance of living in a way which
pleases Him.

If "The Lord is near" (meaning either "immediately
present" or "soon to return"), being anxious ("careful")
does not make sense; once He is in view, things which
seem so critical lose much significance. "Even so,"
someone could say, "Don't worry about anything? How
can anyone stop?"

4:6 "But" can be understood as "instead." Simply stated:
"DON'T WORRY!" Paul offers the alternative to worry:
present every concern to God. "Everything" includes just
that: all matters, small or great.

"Prayer" is meant as the general term for talking with
God; an attitude of reverential communion.

"Petition" is prayer that urges specific action. (Jesus
illustrated this type with His Parable of the Unrighteous
Judge; see Lk. 18:1-8.)

Thanksgiving is an important part of all prayer. By it
Christians recall God's past faithfulness, thus breathing
new hope into their hearts and placing them in a right
relationship with the Father, who deserves constant
praise and gratitude (Rev. 4:11; Rom. 1:21).

4:7 What can the child of God expect as a result? Peace. And
not just the release of getting it off one's chest, but the
peace God gives.

The peace of God is unique, beyond any peace that
could be derived by, say, problem solving. This is not to
suggest that Christians do not seek practical solutions as

do other people. But once that avenue has been explored one can still be left with anxiety: "Did I make the right decision?" The peace that comes after reviewing all the alternatives is not necessarily the same as the peace God gives. "Peace I leave with you; my peace I give you. I do not give to you as the world gives. Do not let your hearts be troubled and do not be afraid" (Jn. 14:27). That peace is uniquely His—unique, also, in its effect.

"This is a picture of a besieged citadel. It is the castle of the mind of the Christian . . . garrisoned strongly. . . . The troops are the Household Guards of the King of Kings and they march behind the standard of the peace of God. Meanwhile, inside the citadel, hearts and thoughts alike are kept in quietness, for their Companion is the King Himself" (Motyer).

4:8   It is not clear whether "finally" is an introduction to the letter's concluding remarks or a connection with the pathway to the peace of God. In either case, verse 8 focuses on several character traits most people admire. Paul teaches that these things should be "thought about" to infuse them into the mind and then the behavior. "Whatever" gives Christians carte blanche in learning from their world and those around them, Christian or not. Wherever and in whomever they discover these traits, they should make their place of study.

"True" implies not only ". . . speaking the truth in love" (Eph. 4:15), but thinking the truth, searching for the truth, admiring and emulating the truth lived out. The real scientist discards wrong hypotheses for ones which more closely fit the facts. Relying on the Spirit's guidance, believers must move from truth to truth, discarding what they learn when it is useless in producing a godly life.

A soldier saves comrades by diving on top of a grenade; a fire fighter rescues a child but forfeits her own life; a passerby prevents a mugging at the risk of serious injury. Most people would agree that these lifesaving actions are dangerous; few would disagree that they should be attempted in spite of that. These acts are "worthy of honor." This is what Paul means by "honest."

"Right" includes not simply what is fair or deserved, but also, as the case may call for it, graciousness in forgiving those who deserve only punishment. As regards dealings with others (relations, employees, slaves, etc.), the word describes scrupulous fairness. The KJV translates: "just."

While Paul surely has sexual chastity in mind when he uses the word "pure," he may also be thinking of single-mindedness and motives untainted by evil intentions.

"Lovely" signifies things that can be loved for themselves by the pure mind. Another word for them is "beautiful," as when we say of an action, "That's beautiful." Things truly beautiful, especially personal traits, induce wonder and calm.

"Admirable" could be rendered "winning" or "gracious." Paul includes those qualities which others recognize and find honorable.

"If" can be understood in two ways: (1) as a condensation of "if there be anything else which has . . ." or (2) "If in the situations you Philippians observe (which display the qualities I listed) you find excellency or praise . . . ." In either case the result is identical: things morally excellent ("virtue") and praiseworthy are to be vigorously thought over, apparently with an eye to imitation.

Below is a list of the key terms in this verse, as they are translated in the KJV. Listed after each term is the word used to translate it in these major translations: New International Version (NIV), Revised Standard Version (RSV), Today's English Version (TEV), Jerusalem Bible (JB), New English Bible (NEB), and J. B. Phillips (JBP). Each item ends with a few other verses in the New Testament in which the word is used.

True—all translations agree. (See also Mt. 22:16; Jn. 7:18; I Jn. 2:27; I Pet. 5:12.)

Honest—"noble" (NIV, TEV, JB, NEB); "honorable" (RSV, JBP) (See also I Tim. 3:8, 11; Titus 2:2—the only other New Testament usages.)

Just—"right" (NIV, TEV); "good" (JB); (See also Mt. 23:35; Acts 4:19; II Thess. 1:5, 6.)

Pure—all translations agree. (See also II Cor. 11:2; I Tim. 5:22; Jas. 3:17; I Jn. 3:3.)

Lovely—"lovable" (NEB); "everything that we love"(JB). (Used only here in the New Testament.)

Of good report—"admirable" (NIV, JBP); "gracious" (RSV, NEB); "honorable" (TEV); "everything that we . . . honour" (JB). (Used only here in the New Testament.)

Virtue—"excellent" (NIV, NEB); "excellence" (RSV); "good" (TEV); "goodness" (JBP); "virtuous" (JB). (See also I Pet. 2:9; II Pet. 1:3, 5 —the only other New Testament usages.)

Praise—"praiseworthy" (NIV); "worthy of praise"(RSV, JB); "things that . . . deserve praise" (TEV); "admirable" (NEB); "approval of God" (JBP). (See also Rom. 2:29; I Cor. 4:5; II Cor. 8:18; I Pet. 2:14.)

In short, as we keep our minds set on what God has given us to do (to bring things into the world that are true, honest, just, and so on), we will find the energy to overcome our self-serving impulses. Psychologist Alfred Adler wrote, "The staking of a goal compels the unity of the personality in that it draws the stream of all spiritual activities into its definite direction."

4:9   The Philippians had received Christian teaching, and had accepted it, but they also had heard and seen certain things in the actions of Paul. Both true information and sound character are on Paul's mind here. We are to do what we see in Paul. It's not enough to only *know* what is right; we must also *do* what is right.

In verses 6 and 7, Paul said to present our requests to God with thanksgiving, and He will give us His peace. Here, Paul suggests that God's peace isn't given automatically. We have a part in the process.

For Discussion

1. What is the practical Christian response to worry and anxiety?

2. How will thinking on the things listed in verse 8 affect a person's daily attitudes? Give some practical examples from your own experience.

3. Compare the world's "peace" and God's "peace." How are they similar? In what ways are they different?

Window on the Word

Saved by the Word

When he landed, or rather, was washed up on shore, Bob knew only that the ship was destroyed and that he was somewhere in the Caribbean.

He regarded himself as an ungrateful self-seeker: he had run away from home, not even leaving a note. And then on his way from Hull to London the ship had capsized in a storm; though he had survived, he had not so much as sent word of his safety to his father or mother.

Now on the island (Despair, he called it) after this second and more disastrous shipwreck, he saw the hand of God against him for his disobedience.

In the course of time he recovered a Bible from the wreck and began to read the New Testament each morning and evening for a little while, meditating on the things of God.

"I found my heart more deeply and sincerely affected with the wickedness of my past life . . . I cried aloud, 'Jesus, thou son of David! Jesus, the exalted Prince and Saviour, give me repentance!' "

He was touched by the power of the Word and saved through it. From then on until his rescue, he lived on the island as a saved man, in communion with God.

Bob's last name? His account bears his name, though the incident of his salvation is commonly deleted from the present abridged forms, except for the 1965 Moody Press edition quoted above.

He was Robinson Crusoe.

13

Thankfulness

Truth to Apply: I know that Christ is the *source* of my power and fulfillment; this gives me joy, and the ability to be thankful, no matter what the circumstances.

Key Verse: For I have learned to be content whatever the circumstances (Phil. 4:11b).

"Just always give thanks," people tell us. But is it really that easy? Being thankful to people can be downright oppressive. We can get so guilty about whether we are thankful enough that we lose the joy of receiving gifts.

Or take the matter of rejoicing. On the one hand, we don't want to glue on a smile and "take everything in stride" in an unruffled way that suggests we cannot feel for people who are suffering. On the other hand, we don't want to take a hopeless, long-faced view about the injustice and corruption that afflict so many.

Can Scripture come to the rescue of people who want to do the right thing and who cannot abide easy answers and cliches? If the Lord wants us to be joyful, will He tell us how?

Background/Overview: *Philippians 4:10-23*

As a prisoner awaiting trial before the emperor, Paul was aware of the possibility of his death. He was also aware of the great ministry responsibilities upon him. Certainly, the Philippian church was dear to him. Paul was thankful for the faith and generosity of the Philippians, and he wanted to let them know this.

Light on the Text

4:10   This verse returns to one of the letter's main burdens: expressing love and appreciation to this church while rejoicing in Christ.

It had been some time since the Philippians had been able to express themselves by a financial gift. They had previously sent the apostle gifts (Phil. 4:15, 16; II Cor. 11:8, 9). Between the time of the earlier gifts and this one, the Philippians had had no opportunity to share with Paul. But since Paul is now a prisoner in Rome, they again manifest their concern and support.

The KJV states that their care of him "hath flourished again." "Flourished" is translated from a word related to horticulture: the care of the Philippians has "blossomed" once more! Paul compares the renewal of their care to the springtime renewal of leaves and flowers. Their concern may have been dormant because external conditions were harsh, but it was far from dead; it was simply awaiting an opportunity.

4:11   Paul shares both his thankfulness to the Philippians and his great joy in their ability and eagerness to offer assistance (see also vss. 17, 18). The apostle does not want to give the impression that he is asking for charity or complaining of need. He has certainly had material needs, but Paul has learned in whatever circumstances he finds himself to be content.

"Content" is a term the Stoic philosophers used for a person who was self-sufficient: "able, by the power of his own will, to resist the shock of circumstance"(M. R. Vincent).

Paul takes this Stoic ideal and shows that it can be fulfilled through Jesus Christ. It isn't Paul's will that fortifies him against the shocks of life—rather it's Christ in him! Just as Christ in you enables you "to resist the shock of circumstance," Christ enables you to be content.

4:12 Paul here shows the practical application of what he has learned in verse 11. Through experience Paul has discovered both how to be humbled by need and how to have plenty without letting that affect his joy. (Read this verse in several Bible translations; see Rom. 8:35-39.)

"Paul is speaking personally in these verses, and he testifies that 'enough' and 'contentment' are relative terms—relative to what we feel ourselves to need. There is a discipline of self whereby one does not need more than one has. . . . Paul says, 'I have made my way up through the degrees of progressive detachment from the things of this world, its comforts and its discomforts alike, and finally I have reached maturity on this point. I know the secret; circumstances can never again touch me.' Thus contentment is the mark of a mature believer, and an objective of all believers who want to grow in Christ . . . ." (Motyer).

So we see that contentment is something that can be learned— "instructed." It is within the grasp and potential of every believer, through the power of the Holy Spirit.

4:13 The sense of this verse is effectively explained by R. P. Martin: ". . . the apostle is insisting that in every conceivable circumstance, 'every where and in all things,' lit., 'in everything and in all things,' he finds the strength (which vital union with Christ supplies) to be adequate for maintaining his apostolic work and for the fulfillment of his desire to accelerate the progress of the Gospel. This statement, then, does not make Paul a wonder-worker, a spiritual 'super-man,' who towers so far above the rest of men that his life is no encouragement to lesser mortals. . . . Here was a man who had boundless confidence in the ability of Christ to match every situation, and whose 'power'. . . is made perfect in his weakness."

As Christians, we, too, can have confidence in the ability of Christ in us to meet every situation. Christ's power is made perfect in our weakness. (See I Timothy 1:12.)

4:14-16 Having protected himself from any taint of covetousness, Paul goes on to heartily thank the Philippians for their fellowship in the spreading of the Gospel. " ' . . . by making common cause with my affliction, by your readiness to share the burden of my troubles.' It was not the actual pecuniary relief, so much as the sympathy and companionship in his sorrow, that the apostle valued" (Lightfoot).

Paul keeps careful note of all transactions, both material and interpersonal. He has an awareness of accounting principles ("giving and receiving"). Apparently, it was Paul's rule not to receive contributions for his ministry. He made an exception in the case of the Philippians.

4:17, 18 Paul again denies any need or coveting of the gift itself. He then returns to the earlier accounting principles ("abound to your account"). He reminds the Philippians that the value of their contributions lay in God's pleasure with them (vss. 17, 18).

Paul gives the Philippians feedback. He provides the "receipt" that he not only has everything he needs, but also is overflowing because of the Philippian's gift brought by Epaphroditus. He commends the Philippians for their generosity, reinforcing a quality important to the Christian. (See Heb. 6:10.)

Paul sees the gift as an offering to God rather than to himself. In this sense, it is "a fragrant offering, an acceptable sacrifice" referring to the ceremonial burnt offerings. (See Gen. 8:21.)

"The burnt offering expresses obedient consecration to God, and God delights in His people dedicated to Himself. Paul teaches here that when Christians take note of Christian needs and generously sacrifice to meet them, it is, for God, the burnt offering all over again, and He delights to accept it" (Motyer).

4:19   Remember that Paul is writing from a prison cell. As
God has provided for all his needs, even through the
Philippians' gift, so, too, God shall provide for all the
saints' needs, through Christ.

"You have supplied all *my* wants (vss. 16, 18), God *on
my behalf* shall supply all *yours*" (Lightfoot).

"He will meet your need to the full. In so doing, His
supply will not be limited to the size of your need, but
rather *according to* (that is, in a manner which befits) *his
riches*" (Motyer).

The key, of course, is Christ. It is in Him that all
riches abound. And it is the Christian's needs that God
will meet in Christ.

4:20   "To our God and Father be glory for ever and ever.
Amen" (RSV). It is only natural for Paul, after bringing
to mind the abundance of riches and grace we have
through Christ Jesus, to burst into a doxology. Note that
here Paul joins himself with the Philippians by saying
"our" God and Father. . . . By the grace of God, all those
who are in Christ Jesus may call God "Father."

4:21-23 A final greeting is extended to the Philippians. The
greeting is sent from the brethren, emphasizing quickly,
once again, the family of God. However, Paul is quick to
include in the family "all the saints," referring especially
to those of "Caesar's household."

Paul ends this letter as he begins, with reference to the
grace bestowed on the Philippians; the grace of Jesus
which, alone, saves us from our sins. When we know this
grace in our own lives and seek to live out the lessons of
Paul's letter to the Philippians, God will restore to us the
joy of our salvation.

For Discussion

1. Although in prison, Paul says he has all he wants or
needs. How can he say that? If Paul is our example, what
does that mean for us today?

2. What is Christian joy? What gets in the way of our
experiencing this joy? How can we experience God's joy

on a regular basis?

3. What does this passage teach about the grace of God? What does the grace of God mean in your own life?

4. What is the secret of contentment? In what ways have you found this contentment in your own life? How do you deal with periods of discontent?

5. A secular song title reads "I Can't Get No Satisfaction." Share your own experience with this feeling. How do you deal with it in light of the Scripture?

Window on the Word

The Presence of Someone

During the long, harrowing trial of eleven Communists, Judge Harold Medina felt strongly that the accused were attempting to wear him down and ruin him.

One day there was pandemonium as all eleven prisoners and some spectators jumped to their feet and lunged shouting toward the judge. But he kept calm, maintained control of the court, and even managed to record some of the indecent language.

Judge Medina later testified: "I tell you that I never had the will and the self-control to do these things. If ever a man felt the presence of someone beside him strengthening his will and giving him aid and comfort, I certainly did that day."

There is One who equips us for anything, granting us His presence and strength when we need it most. For this we may be thankful.

Leader Helps and Lesson Plan

General Guidelines for Group Study

*Open and close each session with prayer.

*Since the lesson texts are not printed in the book, group members should have their Bibles with them for each study session.

*As the leader, prepare yourself for each session through personal study (during the week) of the Bible text and lesson. On notepaper, jot down any points of interest or concern as you study. Jot down your thoughts about how God is speaking to you through the text, and how He might want to speak to the entire group. Look up cross-reference passages (as they are referred to in the lessons), and try to find answers to questions that come to your mind. Also, recall stories from your own life experience that could be shared with the group to illustrate points in the lesson.

*Try to get participation from everyone. Get to know the more quiet members through informal conversation before and after the sessions. Then, during the study, watch for nonverbal signs (a change in expression or posture) that they would like to respond. Call on them. Say: "What are your thoughts on this, Sue?"

*Don't be afraid of silence. Adults need their own space. Often a long period of silence after a question means the group has been challenged to do some real thinking— hard work that can't be rushed!

*Acknowledge each contribution. No question is a dumb question. Every comment, no matter how "wrong," comes from a worthy person, who needs to be affirmed as valuable to the group. Find ways of tactfully accepting the speaker while guiding the discussion back on track: "Thank you for that comment, John; now what do some of the others think?" or, "I see your point, but are you aware of . . . ?"

When redirecting the discussion, however, be sensitive to the fact that sometimes the topic of the moment *should be* the "sidetrack" because it hits a felt need of the participants.

*Encourage *well-rounded* Christian growth. Christians are called to grow in knowledge of the Word, but they are also challenged to grow in love and wisdom. This means that they must constantly develop in their ability to wisely apply the Bible knowledge to their experience.

Lesson Plan

The following four-step lesson plan can be used effectively for each chapter, varying the different suggested approaches from lesson to lesson.

STEP 1: *Focus on Life Need*

The opening section of each lesson is an anecdote, quote, or other device designed to stimulate sharing on how the topic relates to practical daily living. There are many ways to do this. For example, you might list on the chalkboard the group's answers to: "How have you found this theme relevant to your daily life?" "What are your past successes, or failures, in this area?" "What is your present level of struggle or victory with this?" "Share a story from your own experience relating to this topic."

Sharing questions are designed to be open-ended and allow people to talk about themselves. The questions allow for sharing about past experiences, feelings, hopes and dreams, fears and anxieties, faith, daily life, likes and dislikes, sorrows and joys. Self-disclosure results in group members' coming to know each other at a more intimate level. This kind of personal sharing is necessary to experience deep affirmation and love.

However you do it, the point is to get group members to share *where they are now* in relation to the Biblical topic. As you seek to get the group involved, remember the following characteristics of good sharing questions:[1]

1. Good sharing questions encourage risk without forcing participants to go beyond their willingness to respond.

2. Good sharing questions begin with low risk and build toward higher risk. (It is often good, for instance, to ask a history question to start, then build to present situations in people's lives.)

3. Sharing questions should not require people to confess their sins or to share only negative things about themselves.

4. Questions should be able to be answered by every member of the group.

5. The questions should help the group members to know one another better and learn to love and understand each other more.

6. The questions should allow for enough diversity in response so each member does not wind up saying the same thing.

7. They should ask for sharing of self, not for sharing of opinions.

STEP 2: *Focus on Bible Learning*

Use the "Light on the Text" section for this part of the lesson plan. Again, there are a number of ways to get group members involved, but the emphasis here is more on learning Bible content than on applying it. Below are some suggestions on how to proceed. The methods could be varied from week to week.

*Lecture on important points in the Bible passage (from your personal study notes).

*Assign specific verses in the Bible passage to individuals. Allow five or ten minutes for them to jot down 1) questions, 2) comments, 3) points of concern raised by the text. Then have them share in turn what they have written down.

*Pick important or controversial verses from the passage. In advance, do a personal study to find differences of interpretation among commentators. List and explain these "options" on a blackboard and invite comments concerning the relative merits of each view. Summarize and explain your own view, and challenge other group members to further study.

*Have class members do their own outline of the Bible passage. This is done by giving an original title to each section, chapter, and paragraph, placing each under its appropriate heading according to subject matter. Share the outlines and discuss.

*Make up your own sermons from the Bible passage. Each sermon could include: Title, Theme Sentence, Outline, Illustration, Application, Benediction. Share and discuss.

*View works of art based on the text. Discuss.

*Individually, or as a group, paraphrase the Bible passage in your own words. Share and discuss.

*Have a period of silent meditation upon the Bible passage. Later, share insights.

STEP 3: *Focus on Bible Application*

Most adults prefer group discussion above any other learning method. Use the "For Discussion" section for each lesson to guide a good discussion on the lesson topic and how it relates to felt needs.

Students can benefit from discussion in a number of important ways:[2]

1. Discussion stimulates interest and thinking, and helps students develop the skills of observation, analysis, and hope.

2. Discussion helps students clarify and review what they have learned.

3. Discussion allows students to hear opinions that are more mature and perhaps more Christlike than their own.

4. Discussion stimulates creativity and aids students in applying what they have learned.

5. When students verbalize what they believe and are forced to explain or defend what they say, their convictions are strengthened and their ability to share what they believe with others is increased.

There are many different ways to structure a discussion. All have group interaction as their goal. All provide an opportunity to share in the learning process.

But using different structures can add surprise to a discussion. It can mix people in unique ways. It can allow new people to talk.

Total Class Discussion

In some small classes, all students are able to participate in one effective discussion. This can build a sense of class unity, and it allows everyone to hear the wisdom of peers. But in most groups, total class discussion by itself is unsatisfactory because there is usually time for only a few to contribute.

Buzz Groups

Small groups of three to ten people are assigned any topic for discussion. They quickly select a chairperson and a secretary. The chairperson is responsible for keeping the discussion on track, and the secretary records the group's ideas, reporting the relevant ones to the total class.

Brainstorming

Students, usually in small groups, are presented with a problem and asked to come up with as many different solutions as possible. Participants should withhold judgment until all suggestions (no matter how creative!) have been offered. After a short break, the group should pick the best contribution from those suggested and refine it. Each brainstorming group will present its solution in a total class discussion.

Forum Discussion

Forum discussion is especially valuable when the subject is difficult and the students would not be able to participate in a meaningful discussion without quite a bit of background. People with special training or experience have insights which would not ordinarily be available to the students. Each forum member should prepare a three- to five-minute speech and be given uninterrupted time in which to present it. Then students should be encouraged to interact with the speakers, either directly or through a forum moderator.

Debate

As students prepare before class for their parts in a debate, they should remember that it is the affirmative side's repsonsibility to prove that the resolve is correct. The negative has to prove that it isn't. Of course, the negative may also want to present an alternative proposal.

There are many ways to structure a debate, but the following pattern is quite effective.
1. First affirmative speech
2. First negative speech
3. Second affirmative speech
4. Second negative speech
(brief break while each side plans its rebuttal)
5. First negative rebuttal
6. First affirmative rebuttal
7. Second negative rebuttal
8. Second affirmative rebuttal.

Floating Panel

Sometimes you have a topic to which almost everyone in the room would have something to contribute, for example: marriage, love, work, getting along with people. For a change of pace, have a floating panel: four or five people, whose names are chosen at random, will become "experts" for several minutes. These people sit in chairs in the front of the room while you and other class members ask them questions. The questions should be experience related. When the panel has been in front for several minutes, enough time for each person to make several comments, draw other names and replace the original members.

Interview As Homework

Ask students to interview someone during the week and present what they learned in the form of short reports the following Sunday.

Interview in Class

Occasionally it is profitable to schedule an in-class interview, perhaps with a visiting missionary or with someone who has unique insights to share with the group. One person can take charge of the entire interview, structuring and asking questions. But whenever possible the entire class should take part. Each student should write a question to ask the guest.

In-Group Interview

Divide the class into groups of three, called triads. Supply all groups with the same question or discussion topic. A in the group interviews B while C listens. Then B interviews C while A listens. Finally C interviews A while B listens. Each interview should take from one to three minutes. When the triads return to the class, each person reports on what was heard rather than said.

Following every class period in which you use discussion, ask yourself these questions to help determine the success of your discussion time:

1. In what ways did this discussion contribute to the group's understanding of today's lesson?

2. If each person was not involved, what can I do next week to correct the situation?

3. In what ways did content play a role in the discussion? (I.e., people were not simply sharing off-the-top-of-their-head opinions.)

4. What follow-up, if any, should be made on the discussion? (For example, if participants showed a lack of knowledge, or misunderstanding in some area of Scripture, you may want to cover this subject soon during the class hour. Or, if they discussed decisions they were making or projects they felt the class should be involved in, follow-up outside the class hour may be necessary.)

STEP 4: *Focus on Life Response*

This step tries to incorporate a bridge from the Bible lesson to actual daily living. It should be a *specific* suggestion as to "how we are going to *do* something about this," either individually, or as a group. Though this is a goal to aim for, it is unlikely that everyone will respond to every lesson. But it is good to have a suggested life response ready for that one or two in the group who may have been moved by *this* lesson to respond *this week* in a tangible way.

Sometimes a whole group will be moved by one particular lesson to do a major project in light of their deepened understanding of, and commitment to, God's will. Such a response would be well worth the weeks of study that may have preceded it.

Examples of life response activities:

1. A whole class, after studying Scriptural principles of evangelism, decides to host an outreach Bible study in a new neighborhood.

2. As a result of studying one of Paul's prayers for the Ephesians, a group member volunteers to start and oversee a church prayer chain for responding to those in need.

3. A group member invites others to join her in memorizing the key verse for the week.

4. Two group members, after studying portions of the Sermon on the Mount, write and perform a song about peacemaking.

Obviously, only you and your group can decide how to respond appropriately to the challenge of living for Christ daily. But the possibilities are endless.

[1]From *Using the Bible in Groups,* by Roberta Hestenes.
© Roberta Hestenes 1983. Adapted and used by permission of Westminster Press, Philadelphia, PA.
[2]The material on discussion methods is adapted from *Creative Teaching Methods,* by Marlene D. LeFever, available from your local Christian bookstore or from David C. Cook Publishing Co., 850 N. Grove Ave., Elgin, IL 60120. Order number: 25254. $14.95. This book contains step-by-step directions for dozens of methods appropriate for use in adult classes.